ARM 54 Course Guide

Risk Management Principles and Practices
1st Edition

The Institutes
720 Providence Road, Suite 100
Malvern, Pennsylvania 19355-3433

1st Edition • 4th Printing • October 2015

ISBN 978-0-89463-614-1

Contents

 ## Study Materials Available for ARM 54

Risk Management Principles and Practices, 1st ed., 2012, AICPCU.

ARM 54 *Course Guide*, 1st ed., 2012, AICPCU (includes access code for SMART Online Practice Exams).

ARM 54 SMART Study Aids—Review Notes and Flash Cards, 1st ed.

Student Resources

Catalog A complete listing of our offerings can be found in The Institutes' professional development catalog, including information about:

- Current programs and courses
- Current textbooks, course guides, SMART Study Aids, and online offerings
- Program completion requirements
- Exam registration

To obtain a copy of the catalog, visit our website at www.TheInstitutes.org or contact Customer Service at (800) 644-2101.

How to Prepare for Institutes Exams This free handbook is designed to help you by:

- Giving you ideas on how to use textbooks and course guides as effective learning tools
- Providing steps for answering exam questions effectively
- Recommending exam-day strategies

The handbook is printable from the Student Services Center on The Institutes' website at www.TheInstitutes.org or available by calling Customer Service at (800) 644-2101.

Educational Counseling Services To ensure that you take courses matching both your needs and your skills, you can obtain free counseling from The Institutes by:

- Emailing your questions to Advising@TheInstitutes.org
- Calling an Institutes counselor directly at (610) 644-2100, ext. 7601
- Obtaining and completing a self-inventory form, available on our website at www.TheInstitutes.org or by contacting Customer Service at (800) 644-2101

Exam Registration Information As you proceed with your studies, be sure to arrange for your exam.

- Visit our website at www.TheInstitutes.org/forms to access and print the Registration Booklet, which contains information and forms needed to register for your exam.
- Plan to register with The Institutes well in advance of your exam.

How to Contact The Institutes For more information on any of these publications and services:

- Visit our website at www.TheInstitutes.org
- Call us at (800) 644-2101 or (610) 644-2100 outside the U.S.
- Email us at CustomerService@TheInstitutes.org
- Fax us at (610) 640-9576
- Write to us at The Institutes, Customer Service, 720 Providence Road, Suite 100, Malvern, PA 19355-3433

Using This Course Guide

This course guide will help you learn the course content and prepare for the exam.

Each assignment in this course guide typically includes the following components:

Educational Objectives These are the most important study tools in the course guide. Because all of the questions on the exam are based on the Educational Objectives, the best way to study for the exam is to focus on these objectives.

Each Educational Objective typically begins with one of the following action words, which indicate the level of understanding required for the exam:

Analyze—Determine the nature and the relationship of the parts.

Apply—Put to use for a practical purpose.

Associate—Bring together into relationship.

Calculate—Determine numeric values by mathematical process.

Classify—Arrange or organize according to class or category.

Compare—Show similarities and differences.

Contrast—Show only differences.

Define—Give a clear, concise meaning.

Describe—Represent or give an account.

Determine—Settle or decide.

Evaluate—Determine the value or merit.

Explain—Relate the importance or application.

Identify or list—Name or make a list.

Illustrate—Give an example.

Justify—Show to be right or reasonable.

Paraphrase—Restate in your own words.

Recommend—Suggest or endorse something to be used.

Summarize—Concisely state the main points.

Outline The outline lists the topics in the assignment. Read the outline before the required reading to become familiar with the assignment content and the relationships of topics.

Key Words and Phrases These words and phrases are fundamental to understanding the assignment and have a common meaning for those working in insurance. After completing the required reading, test your understanding of the assignment's Key Words and Phrases by writing their definitions.

Review Questions The review questions test your understanding of what you have read. Review the Educational Objectives and required reading, then answer the questions to the best of your ability. When you are finished, check the answers at the end of the assignment to evaluate your comprehension.

Application Questions These questions continue to test your knowledge of the required reading by applying what you've studied to "hypothetical" real-life situations. Again, check the suggested answers at the end of the assignment to review your progress.

Sample Exam Your course guide includes a sample exam (located at the back) or a code for accessing SMART Online Practice Exams (which appears on the inside of the cover). Use the option available for the course you're taking to become familiar with the test format. SMART Online Practice Exams are as close as you can get to experiencing an actual exam before taking one.

More Study Aids

The Institutes also produce supplemental study tools, called SMART Study Aids, for many of our courses. When SMART Study Aids are available for a course, they are listed on page iii of the course guide. SMART Study Aids include Review Notes and Flash Cards and are excellent tools to help you learn and retain the information in each assignment.

About the ARM 54 Exam

The ARM 54 exam contains financially oriented content. Therefore, you will have access to some financial information resources during the exam, as explained in these frequently asked questions:

Q: What resources are available on the computer on which I am taking the exam?

A: During the exam, a reference menu offers access to key financial formulas as well as present value tables.

Q: Which financial formulas are provided on the exam and which formulas do I need to memorize?

A: A list of the formulas provided during the exam is included at the end of this section. The exam provides only the formulas on this list. You must memorize all other necessary formulas.

Q: Which present value tables are included on the exam?

A: A similar version of the present value tables that appear in this course guide are included in the exam. The tables on the exam provide all of the values needed to answer the exam questions.

Q: Can I use a financial calculator while taking the exam?

A: Although a financial calculator is not required for the exam, you are allowed to use any solar or battery powered calculator other than one with alphabetic keys or paper tape. A calculator that permits the input of alphabetic keys (a, b,..., y, z) for the formation of words is not permitted. Any business/financial calculators, including those that are programmable, that meet these criteria are permitted. A financial calculator will not be provided by the testing center.

Q. Can I use a smartphone as a calculator?

A. No, the only electronic device allowed during an exam is a calculator as described in the question above.

Q: To answer questions that ask for present value, do I need to use the formula to calculate the present value factors or can I use the tables that are provided?

A: There are three different methods you can use to determine the correct answer to a present or future value question on the exam:

1. Use a financial calculator.

2. Use the present value tables provided in the exam reference materials to obtain the present value factors used to calculate the answer.

3. Use the formulas provided to calculate the answer.

Using the tables or a financial calculator is much faster than using the formulas.

Q: Are there any common financial calculator mistakes that students often make?

A: Yes, there are some common mistakes that students make when trying to solve ARM 54 exam problems with a financial calculator, including these two:

1. *Trying to learn how to use a financial calculator during the ARM 54 exam*—If you plan on using a financial calculator during the exam, ensure that you know how to use it properly beforehand. You will not be allowed to consult your calculator's user guide during the exam.

2. *Not resetting values*—Most financial calculators store the values entered for present value and future value calculations in their memory. Students who fail to reset these values before each calculation on the exam may find that their incorrect answers are based on values from previous calculations.

Formulas and Tables Accessible During the ARM 54 Exam

The following formulas and tables support calculations, based on the content in Assignment 10, that students will be expected to perform during the ARM 54 exam. They will be provided in a reference menu format during the exam.

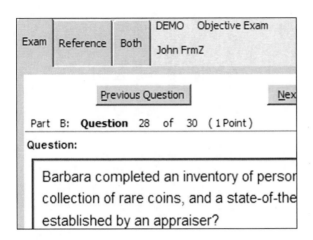

When you reach the first question in Part B of the examination, the Reference Tab will appear in the question screen as shown above. Clicking on the Reference Tab will allow you to access the Formulas and Tables. Learn more about using this feature by running the Tutorial in the examination or in the Demo available online prior to your examination.

Present Value Over a Single or Multiple Periods (Assignment 10)

$$PV = FV_n \div (1 + r)^n$$

where FV_n = future value at the end of n periods, PV = present value or value at the beginning of the period, r = interest rate, and n = number of periods.

Present Value of an Annuity (Assignment 10)

$$PVA = A \times [(1 - (1 \div (1 + r)^n)) \div r]$$

where A = amount of periodic payment.

Net Present Value (Assignment 10)

$$NPV = -C_0 + (C_t \div (1 + r)^t) + \ldots + (C_n \div (1 + r)^n)$$

where C_0 = cash flow at beginning of project, C_t = payment at period t for $t = 1$ through $t = n$, r = discount rate, and n = number of periods.

Present Value Tables (Assignment 10)

Selected PV and PVA factor tables

Note: Examinees may bring their own solar- or battery-powered calculators not equipped with alphabetic keys or paper tape for use during an exam. Business/financial calculators that meet these criteria are also permitted. Although a financial claculator is not required for an exam, use of any solar- or battery-powered calcualtor that does not store alphabetic keys for typing words and that does not contain paper tape is permitted during an exam. Business/financial calculators—including those that are programmable—that meet these criteria are permitted.

Present Value of $1 to Be Received at the End of n Periods $= 1 \div (1 + r)^n$

Interest Rate

Period	1%	2%	3%	4%	5%	6%	7%	8%	9%	10%	12%	14%	16%	18%	20%
1	0.9901	0.9804	0.9709	0.9615	0.9524	0.9434	0.9346	0.9259	0.9174	0.9091	0.8929	0.8772	0.8621	0.8475	0.8333
2	0.9803	0.9612	0.9426	0.9246	0.9070	0.8900	0.8734	0.8573	0.8417	0.8264	0.7972	0.7695	0.7432	0.7182	0.6944
3	0.9706	0.9423	0.9151	0.8890	0.8638	0.8396	0.8163	0.7938	0.7722	0.7513	0.7118	0.6750	0.6407	0.6086	0.5787
4	0.9610	0.9238	0.8885	0.8548	0.8227	0.7921	0.7629	0.7350	0.7084	0.6830	0.6355	0.5921	0.5523	0.5158	0.4823
5	0.9515	0.9057	0.8626	0.8219	0.7835	0.7473	0.7130	0.6806	0.6499	0.6209	0.5674	0.5194	0.4761	0.4371	0.4019
6	0.9420	0.8880	0.8375	0.7903	0.7462	0.7050	0.6663	0.6302	0.5963	0.5645	0.5066	0.4556	0.4104	0.3704	0.3349
7	0.9327	0.8706	0.8131	0.7599	0.7107	0.6651	0.6227	0.5835	0.5470	0.5132	0.4523	0.3996	0.3538	0.3139	0.2791
8	0.9235	0.8535	0.7894	0.7307	0.6768	0.6274	0.5820	0.5403	0.5019	0.4665	0.4039	0.3506	0.3050	0.2660	0.2326
9	0.9143	0.8368	0.7664	0.7026	0.6446	0.5919	0.5439	0.5002	0.4604	0.4241	0.3606	0.3075	0.2630	0.2255	0.1938
10	0.9053	0.8203	0.7441	0.6756	0.6139	0.5584	0.5083	0.4632	0.4224	0.3855	0.3220	0.2697	0.2267	0.1911	0.1615
11	0.8963	0.8043	0.7224	0.6496	0.5847	0.5268	0.4751	0.4289	0.3875	0.3505	0.2875	0.2366	0.1954	0.1619	0.1346
12	0.8874	0.7885	0.7014	0.6246	0.5568	0.4970	0.4440	0.3971	0.3555	0.3186	0.2567	0.2076	0.1685	0.1372	0.1122
13	0.8787	0.7730	0.6810	0.6006	0.5303	0.4688	0.4150	0.3677	0.3262	0.2897	0.2292	0.1821	0.1452	0.1163	0.0935
14	0.8700	0.7579	0.6611	0.5775	0.5051	0.4423	0.3878	0.3405	0.2992	0.2633	0.2046	0.1597	0.1252	0.0985	0.0779
15	0.8613	0.7430	0.6419	0.5553	0.4810	0.4173	0.3624	0.3152	0.2745	0.2394	0.1827	0.1401	0.1079	0.0835	0.0649
16	0.8528	0.7284	0.6232	0.5339	0.4581	0.3936	0.3387	0.2919	0.2519	0.2176	0.1631	0.1229	0.0930	0.0708	0.0541
17	0.8444	0.7142	0.6050	0.5134	0.4363	0.3714	0.3166	0.2703	0.2311	0.1978	0.1456	0.1078	0.0802	0.0600	0.0451
18	0.8360	0.7002	0.5874	0.4936	0.4155	0.3503	0.2959	0.2502	0.2120	0.1799	0.1300	0.0946	0.0691	0.0508	0.0376
19	0.8277	0.6864	0.5703	0.4746	0.3957	0.3305	0.2765	0.2317	0.1945	0.1635	0.1161	0.0829	0.0596	0.0431	0.0313
20	0.8195	0.6730	0.5537	0.4564	0.3769	0.3118	0.2584	0.2145	0.1784	0.1486	0.1037	0.0728	0.0514	0.0365	0.0261
25	0.7798	0.6095	0.4776	0.3751	0.2953	0.2330	0.1842	0.1460	0.1160	0.0923	0.0588	0.0378	0.0245	0.0160	0.0105
30	0.7419	0.5521	0.4120	0.3083	0.2314	0.1741	0.1314	0.0994	0.0754	0.0573	0.0334	0.0196	0.0116	0.0070	0.0042
35	0.7059	0.5000	0.3554	0.2534	0.1813	0.1301	0.0937	0.0676	0.0490	0.0356	0.0189	0.0102	0.0055	0.0030	0.0017
40	0.6717	0.4529	0.3066	0.2083	0.1420	0.0972	0.0668	0.0460	0.0318	0.0221	0.0107	0.0053	0.0026	0.0013	0.0007
50	0.6080	0.3715	0.2281	0.1407	0.0872	0.0543	0.0339	0.0213	0.0134	0.0085	0.0035	0.0014	0.0006	0.0003	0.0001

Present Value of an Annuity of $1 Per Period for n Periods = [1 – (1 ÷ (1 + r)^n)] ÷ r

Interest Rate

Period	1%	2%	3%	4%	5%	6%	7%	8%	9%	10%	12%	14%	16%	18%	20%
1	0.9901	0.9804	0.9709	0.9615	0.9524	0.9434	0.9346	0.9259	0.9174	0.9091	0.8929	0.8772	0.8621	0.8475	0.8333
2	1.9704	1.9416	1.9135	1.8861	1.8594	1.8334	1.8080	1.7833	1.7591	1.7355	1.6901	1.6467	1.6052	1.5656	1.5278
3	2.9410	2.8839	2.8286	2.7751	2.7232	2.6730	2.6243	2.5771	2.5313	2.4869	2.4018	2.3216	2.2459	2.1743	2.1065
4	3.9020	3.8077	3.7171	3.6299	3.5460	3.4651	3.3872	3.3121	3.2397	3.1699	3.0373	2.9137	2.7982	2.6901	2.5887
5	4.8534	4.7135	4.5797	4.4518	4.3295	4.2124	4.1002	3.9927	3.8897	3.7908	3.6048	3.4331	3.2743	3.1272	2.9906
6	5.7955	5.6014	5.4172	5.2421	5.0757	4.9173	4.7665	4.6229	4.4859	4.3553	4.1114	3.8887	3.6847	3.4976	3.3255
7	6.7282	6.4720	6.2303	6.0021	5.7864	5.5824	5.3893	5.2064	5.0330	4.8684	4.5638	4.2883	4.0386	3.8115	3.6046
8	7.6517	7.3255	7.0197	6.7327	6.4632	6.2098	5.9713	5.7466	5.5348	5.3349	4.9676	4.6389	4.3436	4.0776	3.8372
9	8.5660	8.1622	7.7861	7.4353	7.1078	6.8017	6.5152	6.2469	5.9952	5.7590	5.3282	4.9464	4.6065	4.3030	4.0310
10	9.4713	8.9826	8.5302	8.1109	7.7217	7.3601	7.0236	6.7101	6.4177	6.1446	5.6502	5.2161	4.8332	4.4941	4.1925
11	10.3676	9.7868	9.2526	8.7605	8.3064	7.8869	7.4987	7.1390	6.8052	6.4951	5.9377	5.4527	5.0286	4.6560	4.3271
12	11.2551	10.5753	9.9540	9.3851	8.8633	8.3838	7.9427	7.5361	7.1607	6.8137	6.1944	5.6603	5.1971	4.7932	4.4392
13	12.1337	11.3484	10.6350	9.9856	9.3936	8.8527	8.3577	7.9038	7.4869	7.1034	6.4235	5.8424	5.3423	4.9095	4.5327
14	13.0037	12.1062	11.2961	10.5631	9.8986	9.2950	8.7455	8.2442	7.7862	7.3667	6.6282	6.0021	5.4675	5.0081	4.6106
15	13.8651	12.8493	11.9379	11.1184	10.3797	9.7122	9.1079	8.5595	8.0607	7.6061	6.8109	6.1422	5.5755	5.0916	4.6755
16	14.7179	13.5777	12.5611	11.6523	10.8378	10.1059	9.4466	8.8514	8.3126	7.8237	6.9740	6.2651	5.6685	5.1624	4.7296
17	15.5623	14.2919	13.1661	12.1657	11.2741	10.4773	9.7632	9.1216	8.5436	8.0216	7.1196	6.3729	5.7487	5.2223	4.7746
18	16.3983	14.9920	13.7535	12.6593	11.6896	10.8276	10.0591	9.3719	8.7556	8.2014	7.2497	6.4674	5.8178	5.2732	4.8122
19	17.2260	15.6785	14.3238	13.1339	12.0853	11.1581	10.3356	9.6036	8.9501	8.3649	7.3658	6.5504	5.8775	5.3162	4.8435
20	18.0456	16.3514	14.8775	13.5903	12.4622	11.4699	10.5940	9.8181	9.1285	8.5136	7.4694	6.6231	5.9288	5.3527	4.8696
25	22.0232	19.5235	17.4131	15.6221	14.0939	12.7834	11.6536	10.6748	9.8226	9.0770	7.8431	6.8729	6.0971	5.4669	4.9476
30	25.8077	22.3965	19.6004	17.2920	15.3725	13.7648	12.4090	11.2578	10.2737	9.4269	8.0552	7.0027	6.1772	5.5168	4.9789
35	29.4086	24.9986	21.4872	18.6646	16.3742	14.4982	12.9477	11.6546	10.5668	9.6442	8.1755	7.0700	6.2153	5.5386	4.9915
40	32.8347	27.3555	23.1148	19.7928	17.1591	15.0463	13.3317	11.9246	10.7574	9.7791	8.2438	7.1050	6.2335	5.5482	4.9966
50	39.1961	31.4236	25.7298	21.4822	18.2559	15.7619	13.8007	12.2335	10.9617	9.9148	8.3045	7.1327	6.2463	5.5541	4.9995

A

Direct Your Learning ▶▶

Introduction to Risk Management

Educational Objectives

After learning the content of this assignment, you should be able to:

1. Describe risk management and the risk management environment.

2. State the benefits of risk management for an organization and the economy.

3. Summarize various objectives and goals for managing risk.

4. Explain how basic risk measures apply to the management of risk.

5. Explain how the following classifications of risk apply and how they help in risk management:

   - Pure and speculative risk

   - Subjective and objective risk

   - Diversifiable and nondiversifiable risk

   - Quadrants of risk (hazard, operational, financial, and strategic)

6. Describe the concept of enterprise risk management.

Outline

▶ **The Risk Management Environment**
   A. Risk and Risk Management Defined
   B. Risk Management Environment
▶ **Benefits of Risk Management**
   A. Benefits for an Organization
      1. Reduce Cost of Hazard Risk
      2. Reduce Deterrence Effects of Hazard Risks
      3. Reduce Downside Risk
      4. Manage the Downside of Risk
      5. Intelligent Risk Taking
      6. Maximize Profitability
      7. Holistic Risk Management
      8. Legal and Regulatory Requirements
   B. Benefits for the Economy
      1. Reduced Waste of Resources
      2. Improved Allocation of Productive Resources
      3. Reduced Systemic Risk
▶ **Risk Management Objectives and Goals**
   A. Risk Management Objectives
   B. Risk Management Goals
      1. Tolerable Uncertainty
      2. Legal and Regulatory Compliance
      3. Survival
      4. Business Continuity
      5. Earnings Stability
      6. Profitability and Growth
      7. Social Responsibility
      8. Economy of Risk Management Operations
   C. Trade-Offs Among Goals
▶ **Basic Risk Measures**
▶ **Risk Classifications**
   A. Pure and Speculative Risk
   B. Subjective and Objective Risk
   C. Diversifiable and Nondiversifiable Risk
   D. Quadrants of Risk: Hazard, Operational, Financial, and Strategic

▶ **Enterprise Risk Management**
   A. ERM Definitions
   B. Theoretical Pillars of ERM
   C. Organizational Relationships
   D. Implementing ERM
   E. Impediments to ERM

s.m.a.r.t. tips

Don't spend time on material you have already mastered. The SMART Review Notes are organized by the Educational Objectives found in each assignment to help you track your study.

For each assignment, you should define or describe each of the Key Words and Phrases and answer each of the Review and Application Questions.

Educational Objective 1
Describe risk management and the risk management environment.

Key Words and Phrases
Hazard risk

Risk profile

Review Questions

1-1. Compare the traditional concept of risk with the evolved concept of risk.

1-2. Describe the ISO 31000:2009 definition of risk management.

1-3. Describe the holistic approach to risk management.

1-4. Identify the four high-level categories of risk.

1-5. Explain one reason why the evolution of risk management occurred.

1-6. Describe the major changes in the risk landscape.

Application Question

1-7. Using the four high-level categories of risk, categorize these risks:

a.   Cost of materials increases.

b. Competitor hires key employees.

c. United States dollar falls against the euro, making the organization's dollar debts more expensive to pay.

d. There is a fire at a plant.

e. Credit rating is reduced by a credit rating agency, resulting in increased cost of borrowing.

Educational Objective 2
State the benefits of risk management for an organization and the economy.

Key Words and Phrases
Systemic risk

Cost of risk

Review Questions

2-1. Describe how an organization's total cost of risk associated with an asset or activity is calculated.

2-2. Describe three benefits to an organization of reducing deterrence effects by risk management.

2-3. Explain how risk management can help an organization increase intelligent risk taking.

2-4. Explain how risk management can help an organization maximize its profitability.

2-5. Describe the benefits of holistic risk management compared with traditional risk management for an organization.

2-6. Describe three benefits of risk management for the entire economy.

Application Question

2-7. Using the data below, calculate the total cost of risk.

Costs of accidental losses not reimbursed by insurance: $1.2 million

Insurance premiums: $10 million

Risk control techniques: $2 million

Costs of administering risk management activities: $0.5 million

Educational Objective 3
Summarize various objectives and goals for managing risk.

Key Word or Phrase

Value at risk

Review Questions

3-1. Summarize how an organization should align its risk management objectives.

3-2. Explain the risk management goal of tolerable uncertainty.

3-3. Describe the risk management goal of satisfying the organization's legal requirements.

3-4. Summarize the role of risk management in the survival of an organization.

3-5. Identify the steps an organization should take to provide business continuity.

3-6. Explain how risk management helps an organization meet the minimum profit expectation for an activity.

Application Question

3-7. Give an example of how each of the following risk management program goals might conflict with the goal of economy of risk management operations:

a. Tolerable uncertainty

b. Legality

c. Social responsibility

Educational Objective 4
Explain how basic risk measures apply to the management of risk.

Key Words and Phrases

Exposure

Volatility

Law of large numbers

Time horizon

Correlation

Review Questions

4-1. Describe the use of exposure as a risk measure.

4-2. Explain the effect of volatility on risk.

4-3. Describe how consequences are used to measure risk.

4-4. Summarize how the relationship between likelihood and consequences affects risk management.

4-5. Compare the risk related to short and long time horizons.

4-6. Explain the effect of correlation on an organization's risk.

Application Question

4-7. An international manufacturing organization has three major suppliers located in the region of Japan where the 2011 earthquake and tsunami occurred. In 2011, the organization's production was disrupted because supplies could not be received, and this resulted in a loss of sales of $200 million. Explain whether these suppliers present a future risk to the organization according to the basic risk measures that should be managed.

Educational Objective 5

Explain how the following classifications of risk apply and how they help in risk management:

- **Pure and speculative risk**
- **Subjective and objective risk**
- **Diversifiable and nondiversifiable risk**
- **Quadrants of risk (hazard, operational, financial, and strategic)**

Key Words and Phrases

Pure risk

Speculative risk

Credit risk

Subjective risk

Objective risk

Diversifiable risk

Nondiversifiable risk

Market risk

Liquidity risk

Review Questions

5-1. Describe how classifying risk helps an organization's risk management process.

5-2. Compare pure risk with speculative risk.

5-3. Explain why it is important to distinguish between speculative risks and pure risks when making risk management decisions.

5-4. Explain the reasons why subjective and objective risk may differ.

5-5. Contrast diversifiable with nondiversifiable risk.

5-6. Describe the quadrants of risk.

Application Question

5-7. Classify each of these risks as pure or speculative, subjective or objective, and diversifiable or nondiversifiable:

a. Damage to an office building resulting from a hurricane

b. Reduction in value of retirement savings

c. Products liability claim against a manufacturer

Educational Objective 6
Describe the concept of enterprise risk management.

Key Word or Phrase

Enterprise risk management

Review Questions

6-1. Describe a common concept among the various definitions of enterprise risk management (ERM).

6-2. Identify the three theoretical pillars of ERM.

6-3. Compare the traditional risk management function with the ERM risk management function.

6-4. Describe the role of the chief risk officer (CRO) in enterprise risk management.

6-5. Describe communications in an organization with a fully integrated ERM program.

6-6. Provide two typical impediments to successfully implementing an ERM program.

Application Question

6-7. An organization manufactures and sells nonprescription pain-relief products. There is a products liability risk associated with this business. Describe a traditional risk management approach to this risk versus an ERM approach.

Answers to Assignment 1 Questions

NOTE: These answers are provided to give students a basic understanding of acceptable types of responses. They often are not the only valid answers and are not intended to provide an exhaustive response to the questions.

Educational Objective 1

1-1. The traditional concept of risk, inherent to insurance, is that risk is a hazard that could happen to an individual or organization. The evolved concept of risk as "the effect of uncertainty on objectives" provides a much broader understanding.

1-2. The ISO 31000:2009 definition of risk management is "coordinated activities to direct and control an organization with regard to risk." This definition reflects an organization managing risks, both positive and negative, to meet its objectives.

1-3. Recent risk management theory includes the concept of a holistic approach to risk management. Organizations now realize that it is important to manage all of their risks, not just those that are familiar or easy to quantify. Risks that seem insignificant have the potential to create significant damage or opportunity when they interact with other events. A holistic approach helps organizations to develop a true perspective on the significance of various risks.

1-4. These are the high-level categories of risk:

- Hazard (or pure) risks

- Operational risks

- Financial risks

- Strategic risks

1-5. The evolution of risk management has occurred in part because of high-profile failures of large organizations during the late twentieth and early twenty-first century, followed by the global financial crisis.

1-6. In large part because of trends in technology, globalization, and finance, the risk landscape has changed dramatically. Organizations operate in a global environment where they face hazard risks such as earthquakes and floods, political risks such as terrorism, economic risks such as a recession, and financial risk such as currency exchange rates. Interconnection of these risks adds to their complexity and potential effect on organizations.

1-7. The described risks are categorized in this manner:

a. Financial risk

b. Strategic risk

c. Financial risk

d. Hazard risk

e. Financial risk

Educational Objective 2

2-1. An organization's cost of risk associated with an asset or activity is the total of these:

- Costs of accidental losses not reimbursed by insurance or other outside sources

- Insurance premiums or expenses incurred for noninsurance indemnity

- Costs of risk control techniques to prevent or reduce the size of accidental losses

- Costs of administering risk management activities

2-2. Risk management reduces the deterrence effects of uncertainty about potential future accidental losses by making these losses less frequent, less severe, or more foreseeable. The resulting reduction in uncertainty benefits an organization in these ways:

- Alleviates or reduces management's fears about potential losses, thereby increasing the feasibility of ventures that once appeared too risky

- Increases profit potential by greater participation in investment or production activities

- Makes the organization a safer investment and, therefore, more attractive to suppliers of investment capital through which the organization can expand

2-3. A benefit of risk management includes providing the organization with a framework to analyze the risks associated with an opportunity and then to manage those risks. Risk management can help the organization decide if the potential rewards are greater than the downside risks, thereby increasing intelligent risk taking.

2-4. Risk management can help an organization maximize its profitability by providing it with information to evaluate the potential risk-adjusted return on its activities and to manage the risks associated with those activities. Although the same amount of capital may be required for each activity being considered, the risk-adjusted return will not be the same. Risk managers can help the organization evaluate the risks and potential returns of its activities and how these activities will affect the organization's efforts to meet its objectives.

2-5. Traditional risk management was conducted in silos within an organization. This fragmented approach can miss critical risks to the organization and fails to provide senior management with a picture of the organization's risk portfolio and profile. An integrated, holistic approach that manages risk across all levels and functions within an organization presents a more complete picture of an organization's risk portfolio and profile. This picture allows for better decisions by and improved outcomes for senior management.

2-6. Risk management benefits the entire economy by reducing waste of resources, improving allocation of productive resources, and reducing systemic risk.

Any economy possesses a given quantity of resources with which to produce goods and services. If an accidental loss reduces those resources, such as when a fire or an earthquake demolishes a factory or destroys a highway, that economy's overall productive resources are reduced. Risk management prevents or minimizes the waste of these productive resources.

Risk management also improves the allocation of productive resources because, when economic uncertainty is reduced for individual organizations, allocating productive resources is improved.

The benefits of risk-management programs at systemically important organizations include reducing systemic risk and reassuring investors and the public about reasonable risk taking that can provide economic growth.

2-7. The total cost of risk is calculated in this way:

$1.2 million + $10 million + $2 million + $0.5 million = $13.7 million

Educational Objective 3

3-1. Each organization should align its risk management objectives with its overall objectives. These objectives should reflect the organization's risk appetite and the organization's internal and external context.

3-2. A typical risk management goal is tolerable uncertainty, which means aligning risks with the organization's risk appetite. Managers want to be assured that whatever might happen will be within the bounds of what was anticipated and will be effectively addressed by the risk management program. Risk management programs should use measurements that align with the organization's overall objectives and take into account the risk appetite of senior management.

3-3. An important goal for risk management programs is to ensure that the organization's legal obligations are satisfied. Such legal obligations are typically based on these items:

- Standard of care that is owed to others

- Contracts entered into by the organization

- Federal, state, provincial, territorial, and local laws and regulations

3-4. Survival of an organization depends on identifying as many risks as possible that could threaten the organization's ability to survive and managing those risks appropriately. It also depends on anticipating and recognizing emerging risks.

3-5. These are the steps an organization should take to provide business continuity and, therefore, resiliency:

- Identify activities whose interruptions cannot be tolerated

- Identify the types of accidents that could interrupt such activities

- Determine the standby resources that must be immediately available to counter the effects of those accidents

- Ensure the availability of the standby resources at even the most unlikely and difficult times

3-6. To achieve that minimum amount, risk management professionals must identify the risks that could prevent this goal from being reached, as well as the risks that could help achieve this goal within the context of the organization's overall objectives.

3-7. The risk management program goal of economy of operations conflicts with other risk management goals in these ways:

a.   Tolerable uncertainty might conflict with the goal of economy of operations because of the cost of risk management efforts.

b. Legality might conflict with the goal of economy of operations because implementing safety standards could be an added expense.

c. Social responsibility might conflict with the goal of economy of operations because obligations such as charitable contributions could raise costs.

Educational Objective 4

4-1. Exposure provides a measure of the maximum potential damage associated with an occurrence. Generally, the risk increases as the exposure increases, assuming the risk is nondiversifiable.

4-2. Volatility provides a basic measure that can be applied to risk. Generally, risk increases as volatility increases.

4-3. Consequences are the measure of the degree to which an occurrence could positively or negatively affect an organization. The greater the consequences, the greater the risk.

4-4. The relationship between likelihood and consequences is critical for risk management in assessing risk and deciding whether and how to manage it. Therefore, organizations must determine to the extent possible the likelihood of an event and then determine the potential consequences if the event occurs. In assessing the level of risk, the risk management professional must understand to the extent possible both the likelihood and the consequences.

4-5. Longer time horizons are generally riskier than shorter ones.

4-6. Correlation is a measure that should be applied to the management of an organization's overall risk portfolio. If two or more risks are similar, they are usually highly correlated. The greater the correlation, the greater the risk.

4-7. The organization has risk from exposure, consequences, and correlation related to these suppliers. The consequences to the organization of disruption to the supply chain were lost sales of $200 million. The maximum exposure and consequences are unknown and depend on the length of any future disruption. The organization's risk management professionals should quantify to the extent possible the probable range of exposure and consequences. There is correlation because the three suppliers are in the same area. Although the likelihood of another earthquake and tsunami is not high, the potential consequences, were they to occur, are high. Therefore, this risk should be managed.

Educational Objective 5

5-1. Classification can help with assessing risks, because many risks in the same classification have similar attributes. It also can help with managing risk, because many risks in the same classification can be managed with similar techniques. Finally, classification helps with the administrative function of risk management by helping to ensure that risks in the same classification are less likely to be overlooked.

5-2. A pure risk is a chance of loss or no loss, but no chance of gain. In comparison, speculative risk involves a chance of gain.

5-3. It is important for an organization to distinguish between speculative risks and pure risks when making risk management decisions because the two types of risk must often be managed differently. Further, most insurance policies are not designed to handle speculative risks.

5-4. Subjective and objective risk may differ for these reasons:

- Familiarity and control—For example, although many people consider air travel (over which they have no control) to carry a high degree of risk, they are much more likely to suffer a serious injury when driving their cars, where the perception of control is much greater.

- Consequences over likelihood—People often have two views of low-likelihood, high-consequence events. The first misconception is the "It can't happen to me" view, which assigns a probability of zero to low-likelihood events such as natural disasters, murder, fires, accidents, and so on. The second misconception is overstating the probability of a low-likelihood event, which is common for people who have personally been exposed to the event previously. If the effect of a particular event can be severe, such as the potentially destructive effects of a hurricane or earthquake, the perception of the frequency of deaths resulting from such an event is heightened. This perception may be enhanced by the increased media coverage given to high-severity events.

- Risk awareness—Organizations differ in terms of their level of risk awareness and, therefore, perceive risks differently. An organization that is not aware of its risks would perceive the likelihood of something happening as very low.

5-5. Diversifiable risk is not highly correlated and can be managed through diversification, or spread, of risk. Nondiversifiable risks are correlated—that is, their gains or losses tend to occur simultaneously rather than randomly.

5-6. One approach to categorizing risks involves dividing them into these risk quadrants:

- Hazard risks arise from property, liability, or personnel loss exposures and are generally the subject of insurance.

- Operational risks fall outside the hazard risk category and arise from people or a failure in processes, systems, or controls.

- Financial risks arise from the effect of market forces on financial assets or liabilities and include market risk, credit risk, liquidity risk, and price risk.

- Strategic risks arise from trends in the economy and society, including changes in the economic, political, and competitive environments, as well as from demographic shifts.

5-7. These answers classify the described risks:

a. The risk of hurricane damage to an office building is a pure risk in that there is no chance of gain from the damage. The risk is both subjective and objective. The building owner may have his or her own idea about the frequency or severity of loss (subjective), and there are objective measures of frequency and severity based on historical data or catastrophe modeling. Hurricane damage to an office building is usually nondiversifiable because hurricanes affect many properties simultaneously.

b. The reduction in value of retirement savings is a speculative risk because there is a chance of loss, no loss, or gain. The risk is both subjective and objective. The investor may have his or her own expectations of retirement investments (subjective), as well as historical data (objective) on investment returns. The risk is diversifiable because the investor has many investment options to offset the risk of a reduction in retirement savings.

      c.   A products liability claim against a manufacturer is a pure risk, both subjective and objective, and diversifiable. The manufacturer can diversify into other products or services to reduce its exposure to products liability claims.

Educational Objective 6

6-1. The various definitions of ERM all include the concept of managing all of an organization's risks to help an organization meet its objectives. This link between the management of an organization's risks and its objectives is a key driver in deciding how to assess and treat risks.

6-2. Three main theoretical concepts explain how ERM works:

- Interdependency

- Correlation

- Portfolio theory

6-3. Under the traditional risk management organizational model, there is a risk manager and a risk management department to manage hazard risk. This traditional function mainly provides risk transfer, such as insurance, for the organization. In ERM, the responsibility of the risk management function is broader and includes all of an organization's risks, not just hazard risk. Additionally, the entire organization at all levels becomes responsible for risk management as the ERM framework encompasses all stakeholders.

6-4. As facilitator, the CRO engages the organization's management in a continuous conversation that establishes risk strategic goals in relationship to the organization's strengths, weaknesses, opportunities, and threats (SWOT). The CRO's responsibility includes helping the enterprise to create a risk culture in which managers of the organization's divisions and units, and eventually individual employees, become risk owners.

6-5. An organization with a fully integrated ERM program develops a communication matrix that moves information throughout the organization. Communications include dialogue and discussions among the different units and levels within the organization. The establishment of valid metrics and the continuous flow of cogent data are a critical aspect to this communication process. The metrics are carefully woven into reporting structures that engage the entire organization, including both internal and external stakeholders.

6-6. An impediment to successfully adopting ERM is technological deficiency. Another and perhaps the single largest impediment to successful implementation of ERM is the traditional organization culture with its entrenched silos.

6-7. A traditional risk management approach would be to apply risk control techniques in the manufacture and distribution of this product and to purchase liability insurance to transfer some of the liability exposure related to consumers' use of the product. An ERM approach would, in addition to risk control and risk transfer techniques, also address the reputational risk related to product liability and the potential loss of business income if a particular product is removed from the market.

Direct Your Learning

Risk Management Standards and Guidelines

Educational Objectives

After learning the content of this assignment, you should be able to:

1. Describe the general characteristics and elements of risk management standards and guidelines.

2. Explain how ISO 31000 provides a framework and a process for an organization to manage its risks.

3. Explain how the Committee of Sponsoring Organizations' Enterprise Risk Management—Integrated Framework provides a standard by which an organization can manage its risks.

4. Explain how the Solvency II and Basel II and III regulatory standards apply to the insurance and banking industries, respectively.

Outline

▶ **Introduction to Risk Management Standards and Guidelines**
  A. The Nature of Standards and Guidelines
  B. Common Elements of Risk Management Standards
  C. Summary of the Major Standards and Guidelines

▶ **ISO 31000 Risk Management—Principles and Guidelines**
  A. Background
  B. Scope
  C. Principles
  D. Framework
  E. Process
    1. Risk Assessment
    2. Risk Treatment
    3. Risk Monitoring and Review

▶ **COSO Enterprise Risk Management—Integrated Framework**
  A. Background
  B. Framework
  C. Control Activities

▶ **Solvency II and Basel II and III Regulatory Standards**
  A. Solvency II
  B. Basel II and III

 Reduce the number of Key Words and Phrases that you must review. SMART Flash Cards contain the Key Words and Phrases and their definitions, allowing you to set aside those cards that you have mastered.

For each assignment, you should define or describe each of the Key Words and Phrases and answer each of the Review and Application Questions.

Educational Objective 1
Describe the general characteristics and elements of risk management standards and guidelines.

Key Words and Phrases

Risk management standard

Framework

Review Questions

1-1. Describe a risk management standard.

1-2. Describe the common purpose of all risk management standards.

1-3.   Contrast the ISO 31000 and the COSO definitions of risk.

1-4.   Identify the criteria that should be used to select a risk management standard.

1-5.   Explain what frameworks and standards provide to an organization.

1-6.   Describe the purpose of the Risk and Insurance Management Society's Risk Maturity Model (RMM).

Application Question

1-7. Laura is the newly hired risk manager for a mid-size manufacturing organization. Previously, the organization focused only on hazard risk and risk management. Explain why Laura would recommend using an internationally recognized risk management standard for its risk management program.

Educational Objective 2

Explain how ISO 31000 provides a framework and a process for an organization to manage its risks.

Key Words and Phrases

Risk management framework

Risk criteria

Review Questions

2-1. Explain whether the ISO 31000 risk management standard is designed to produce uniformity.

2-2. Describe in general what a risk management policy should address.

2-3. Identify the three processes included in the ISO 31000 definition of risk assessment.

2-4. Describe risk treatment in the ISO 31000 risk management standard.

2-5. Describe the monitoring phase of the ISO 31000 risk management standard.

Educational Objective 3

Explain how the Committee of Sponsoring Organizations' Enterprise Risk Management—Integrated Framework provides a standard by which an organization can manage its risks.

Key Words and Phrases

Inherent risk

Residual risk

Review Questions

3-1. Describe how the Committee of Sponsoring Organizations (COSO) defines risk.

3-2. Identify the four categories in which the COSO Enterprise Risk Management—Integrated Framework is intended to help an organization achieve its objectives.

3-3. Explain how the COSO risk management framework should be applied across an organization.

3-4.   Explain why control activities are a key feature of the COSO Enterprise Risk Management—Integrated Framework.

3-5.   Describe control activities in the COSO Enterprise Risk Management—Integrated Framework.

3-6.   Explain the two types of monitoring of control activities in the COSO Enterprise Risk Management—Integrated Framework.

Application Question

3-7.   A risk manager is developing a control activity for a bank's mortgage underwriting. The bank's objective is that all mortgages conform to guidelines. Explain the control activity the risk manager might develop and how compliance would be determined.

Educational Objective 4

Explain how the Solvency II and Basel II and III regulatory standards apply to the insurance and banking industries, respectively.

Key Words and Phrases

Risk-based capital (RBC)

Modeling

Review Questions

4-1. Identify the areas in which Solvency II aims to achieve consistency across Europe.

4-2. Describe the three supporting pillars of Solvency II.

4-3. Compare the effects of Solvency II on European insurers with those on United States insurers.

4-4. Describe the three pillars of the Basel Capital Adequacy Framework.

4-5. Explain the purpose of Basel III.

4-6. Identify the processes that the Basel Committee states are encompassed by risk management.

Application Question

4-7. Although Solvency II poses a number of new requirements for European insurers, what is an advantage that some insurers could receive from Solvency II?

Answers to Assignment 2 Questions

NOTE: These answers are provided to give students a basic understanding of acceptable types of responses. They often are not the only valid answers and are not intended to provide an exhaustive response to the questions.

Educational Objective 1

1-1. A risk management standard can be understood as defining the risk management process together with the framework that will be applied to the process. The framework is the structure that supports the organization's objectives and strategies. It provides the scaffold that an organization uses to construct and maintain its risk management process.

1-2. All of the standards share a common purpose of helping organizations assess and manage risk.

1-3. The COSO definition is "the possibility that an event will occur and adversely affect the achievement of objectives." This definition reflects the traditional meaning of risk—namely, that it represents the potential only for adverse results. The ISO 31000 definition of risk is "the effect of uncertainty on objectives." This definition reflects more recent thinking about risk, which encompasses the potential for positive as well as adverse results.

1-4. For the risk management process to be implemented successfully, the standard(s) should be selected based on these criteria:

- Alignment with organizational objectives

- Adherence to controls

- Need to meet regulatory requirements (compliance)

- Risk governance

1-5. Frameworks and standards provide an organization with approaches for identifying, analyzing, responding to, and monitoring risks (threats and opportunities) within the internal and external contexts in which it operates. Compliance with the assumed best practices represented by the standards, including the frameworks, demonstrates that an organization is properly managing risk.

1-6. The RMM is an objective and consistent measurement tool for an organization to use to conduct periodic self-assessments. It focuses on seven essential attributes:

- ERM-based approach

- ERM process management

- Risk appetite management

- Root cause discipline

- Uncovering risks

- Performance management

- Business resiliency and sustainability

Key drivers of each attribute are analyzed and measured to establish the maturity level. The organization bases its self-assessment on its performance in these attributes along a maturity continuum ranging from nonexistent at level zero to leadership at level five.

1-7. Laura would recommend a risk management standard to provide the framework and process that could be used to manage all of the organization's risk, including positive as well as negative risk. She would recommend a standard to align with the organization's objectives, provide controls, satisfy regulatory requirements, and provide risk governance. She would also recommend a standard to establish best practices and to provide common terminology for external discussions.

Educational Objective 2

2-1. Although the ISO 31000 standard is universally applicable, it is not intended to produce uniformity. On the contrary, its emphasis is on tailoring a process and framework to an individual organization's needs.

2-2. A risk management policy should address how the organization will identify risks and how it will measure, review, and communicate its risk management efforts.

2-3. The three processes included in the ISO 31000 definition of risk assessment are risk identification, risk analysis, and risk evaluation.

2-4. ISO 31000 describes risk treatment as the ongoing process of deciding on an option for modifying risk and whether the residual level of risk is acceptable, selecting a new risk treatment if the current one is not effective, and then repeating this assessment.

2-5. ISO 31000 asserts that monitoring and reviewing both internal and external changes and how these changes affect risks and their treatment should be a planned part of the risk management process. Monitoring should also include recording the assessments and reporting them internally and externally, as needed; further, determining the frequency, distribution, and method of reporting is an integral part of developing the risk management process.

Educational Objective 3

3-1. COSO defines risk as the possibility that an event will occur and adversely affect an organization's objectives.

3-2. The COSO Enterprise Risk Management—Integrated Framework is designed to help an organization achieve its objectives in four categories:

- Strategic—high-level goals, aligned with and supporting its mission
- Operations—effective and efficient use of its resources
- Reporting—reliability of reporting
- Compliance—compliance with applicable laws and regulations

3-3. COSO states that "risk management is not strictly a serial process, where one component affects only the next. It is a multidirectional...process in which almost any component can and does influence another." The process should be applied across all four levels of an organization: entity, division, business unit, and subsidiary.

3-4. Because COSO 2004 historically focused on financial controls and developed its risk management framework in the context of internal audits related to compliance with Sarbanes-Oxley, control activities are a key feature of this standard in comparison with other risk management standards.

3-5. Control activities are policies and procedures applied to each of the four categories of objectives—strategic, operations, reporting, and compliance. Control activities typically have two parts. The first part is the policy that states what should be done, and the second part is the procedure to accomplish the policy.

3-6. There are two types of monitoring. The first type is ongoing regular monitoring by an organization's management. The second type is periodic evaluation, often by internal auditors. Internal auditors can identify areas where control activities are deficient and make recommendations to improve them.

3-7. The control activity should have a policy and procedure. The policy would be that all mortgages conform to guidelines. The procedure would be generating reports based on the mortgage information entered into the bank's computer system. Compliance would be determined by periodic monitoring of the reports by risk management and by internal auditors.

Educational Objective 4

4-1. Solvency II aims to achieve consistency across Europe in these areas:

- Market-consistent balance sheets

- Risk-based capital

- Own risk and solvency assessment (ORSA)

- Senior management accountability

- Supervisory assessment

4-2. Solvency II contains three supporting pillars:

- Pillar 1—This pillar covers all the financial requirements and aims to ensure firms are adequately capitalized with risk-based capital. It includes the use of internal models that, subject to stringent standards and prior supervisory approval, enable a firm to calculate its regulatory capital requirements using its own internal modeling.

- Pillar 2—This pillar imposes higher standards of risk management and governance within an organization and gives supervisors greater powers to challenge their firms on risk management issues. The ORSA requires a firm to undertake its own forward-looking self-assessment of its risks, corresponding capital requirements, and adequacy of capital resources.

- Pillar 3—This pillar aims for greater levels of transparency for supervisors and the public. There is a private annual report by insurers to supervisors and a public solvency and financial condition report that increases the required level of disclosure.

4-3. European insurers are required to have an effective risk management system, conduct their own risk and solvency assessment, have an effective internal control system in place, and provide for an effective internal audit function and an effective actuarial function.

The most immediate effect is on United States insurers that have subsidiaries in European countries that will be subject to Solvency II. It is expected that U.S. insurers with no European subsidiaries will be granted regulatory equivalency status under Solvency II.

4-4. The Capital Adequacy Framework consists of three pillars:

- Minimum capital requirements—Refinement of the standardized rules in the 1988 Accord that set out specific weights for different types of credit risk, such as government bonds and mortgages. Basel II offered more sophisticated alternatives for evaluating credit risk, such as evaluations of a borrower's credit rating. The minimum capital standard, however, remained at 8 percent.

- Supervisory—Review of an institution's internal assessment process and capital adequacy.

- Disclosure—Effective use of disclosure to strengthen market discipline and complement supervisory efforts. The Basel Committee states that "Market discipline imposes strong incentives on banks to conduct their business in a safe, sound and efficient manner, including an incentive to maintain a strong capital base as a cushion against potential future losses arising from risk exposures."

4-5. Basel III is a revised standard in response to the financial crisis that began in 2007. The Basel Committee on Banking Supervision developed this standard to address both the risk of individual organizations and systemic risk. Basel III is a comprehensive set of reform measures to strengthen the regulation, supervision, and risk management of the banking sector.

4-6. The Basel Committee states that risk management encompasses these processes:

- Identifying risks to a bank

- Measuring exposures to those risks where possible

- Ensuring that an effective capital planning and monitoring program is in place

- Monitoring risk exposures and corresponding capital needs on an ongoing basis

- Taking steps to control or mitigate risk exposures, and reporting to senior management and the board on the bank's risk exposures and capital positions

4-7. Insurers that can demonstrate a strong risk management standard, including framework, process, and monitoring, may have an opportunity to reduce capital requirements.

Direct Your Learning

Hazard Risk

Educational Objectives

After learning the content of this assignment, you should be able to:

1. Describe hazard risk and its treatment.

2. Describe the following elements for property, liability, personnel, and net income loss exposures:

    - Assets exposed to loss

    - Causes of loss, including associated hazards

    - Financial consequences of loss

3. Summarize the loss exposures addressed by each of the various commercial insurance policies.

Outline

▶ **The Nature of Hazard Risk**
   A. Definition of Hazard Risk
   B. Measuring and Managing Hazard Risk
   C. The Role of Insurance
▶ **Loss Exposures**
   A. Elements of Loss Exposures
      1. Asset Exposed to Loss
      2. Cause of Loss
      3. Financial Consequences of Loss
   B. Types of Loss Exposures
      1. Property Loss Exposures
      2. Liability Loss Exposures
      3. Personnel Loss Exposures
      4. Net Income Loss Exposures
▶ **Commercial Insurance Policies**
   A. Classifying Commercial Insurance Policies
   B. Property Insurance
      1. Business Income Insurance
      2. Industrial All-Risk (Special Risk) Insurance
      3. Builders' All-Risk Insurance
      4. Equipment Breakdown (Boiler & Machinery) Insurance
   C. Fidelity and Crime Insurance
   D. Surety Bonds
   E. General Liability Insurance
   F. Auto Insurance
   G. Workers Compensation and Employers Liability Insurance
   H. Professional Liability or Errors and Omissions Insurance
   I. Management Liability Insurance
      1. Directors and Officers Liability Insurance
      2. Employment Practices Liability
      3. Fiduciary Liability
   J. Aircraft Insurance
   K. Ocean Marine Insurance
   L. Environmental Insurance

s.m.a.r.t.® tips   Actively capture information by using the open space in the SMART Review Notes to write out key concepts. Putting information into your own words is an effective way to push that information into your memory.

For each assignment, you should define or describe each of the Key Words and Phrases and answer each of the Review and Application Questions.

Educational Objective 1
Describe hazard risk and its treatment.

Key Words and Phrases

Frequency

Severity

Avoidance

Separation

Duplication

Diversification

Insurance

Review Questions

1-1. Describe the three major categories of hazard risk.

1-2. Contrast net income losses associated with property and liability losses.

1-3. Identify the two measures that are traditionally used for hazard risk exposures.

1-4. Explain how the measurement of hazard risk can assist risk managers in determining whether to retain or transfer risk.

1-5. Provide two advantages of risk transfer.

1-6.   Describe limitations to the risk transfer provided by insurance.

Application Question

1-7.   Identify which risk management technique is used in each of the following examples.

   a.   A pharmaceutical company decides not to manufacture a drug because of its potential side effects.

   b.   An insurer decides to increase its personal auto line of business because of its shorter time horizon for losses than its commercial liability business.

   c.   A transport company begins a driver safety program.

d. A warehouse owner installs a sprinkler system that will be activated in the event of fire.

Educational Objective 2

Describe the following elements for property, liability, personnel, and net income loss exposures:

- **Assets exposed to loss**
- **Causes of loss, including associated hazards**
- **Financial consequences of loss**

Key Words and Phrases

Loss exposure

Hazard

Moral hazard

Morale hazard (attitudinal hazard)

Physical hazard

Legal hazard

Property loss exposure

Tangible property

Real property (realty)

Personal property

Intangible property

Liability loss exposure

Personnel loss exposure

Personal loss exposure

Net income loss exposure

Review Questions

2-1. List three elements necessary to describe a loss exposure.

2-2. Identify types of assets that could be loss exposures for these entities:

    a. Organization's assets

    b. Individual's assets

2-3. Describe the four classifications of hazards.

2-4. Identify three factors that affect the financial consequences of a loss.

2-5. Distinguish between these types of property:

   a. Tangible property

   b. Intangible property

   c. Real property

   d. Personal property

2-6. Explain how an organization or individual might experience a financial loss
      from these types of loss exposures:

   a. Property loss exposure

   b. Liability loss exposure

   c. Personnel loss exposure

   d. Net income loss exposure

Application Question

2-7. ABC's Used Cars, Inc. (ABC) has applied for property and liability insurance. Describe a possible hazard that ABC might face in each of these categories: (Answers may vary.)

a. Moral hazard

b. Morale hazard

c. Physical hazard

d. Legal hazard

Educational Objective 3
Summarize the loss exposures addressed by each of the various commercial insurance policies.

Key Words and Phrases

Property-casualty insurance

Property

Liability

Line of business

Commercial property insurance

Monoline policy

Package policy

Named peril

Direct physical loss

All-risks policy

Bailees' customers policy

Replacement cost

Actual cash value

Insurance-to-value provision

Coinsurance clause

Business income insurance

Dependent property exposure

Principal

Surety

Obligee

Tort

Breach of contract

Insuring agreement

Occurrence

Indemnify

Claims-made coverage form

Occurrence coverage form

Entity coverage

Claims-made coverage trigger

Fiduciary liability insurance

Perils of the sea

Review Questions

3-1. Compare named perils to direct physical loss coverage.

3-2. Summarize the type of coverage provided by business income insurance.

3-3. Identify three unique characteristics of builders' risk.

3-4. Explain what distinguishes liability from other types of loss exposures and the purpose of general liability insurance.

3-5. Describe directors and officers (D&O) insurance coverage.

3-6. Identify the three characteristics of aviation loss exposures that distinguish them from other types of loss exposures.

3-7. Explain why a risk manager for a United States organization might recommend the purchase of an environmental liability policy.

▶▶

Answers to Assignment 3 Questions

NOTE: These answers are provided to give students a basic understanding of acceptable types of responses. They often are not the only valid answers and are not intended to provide an exhaustive response to the questions.

Educational Objective 1

1-1. Hazard risk can be categorized in this manner:

- Personnel risk—Uncertainty related to the loss to a firm due to death, incapacity, loss of health, or prospect of harm to or unexpected departure of key employees.

- Property risk—Uncertainty related to loss of wealth due to damage or destruction of property.

- Liability risk—Uncertainty related to financial responsibility arising from bodily injury (including death) or loss of wealth that a person or an entity causes to others.

1-2. Unlike the net income losses associated with property losses, no definite time period is associated with liability losses. There is no way to set a reasonable time period to restore a business's related income after a liability loss in a similar manner to the restoration of a business's property.

1-3. The two measures that are traditionally used for hazard risk exposures are frequency and severity. An organization's risk managers should measure frequency and severity on an aggregate basis by line of insurance annually.

1-4. Loss measurement will assist the risk manager in recommending which losses should be retained and which should be transferred. Typically, losses with low frequency and severity are retained. Some losses with high frequency but low severity may also be retained, because the aggregate results are usually fairly predictable. Losses with high severity but low frequency are often transferred. Most organizations would avoid losses with high frequency and severity.

1-5. The principal advantage of risk transfer is that it provides an offset to an organization's exposure to large losses. Additionally, risk transfer can lessen the variability of the cash flows of an organization.

1-6. There are several significant limitations to the risk transfer provided by insurance. In addition to deductibles and self-insured retentions, there are also policy limits for most lines of insurance that may not provide sufficient coverage in the event of a large loss. Additionally, most policies exclude certain types of exposures.

1-7. These answers relate to the identification of risk management technique.

a. The company is using the technique of avoidance.

b. The insurer is using the technique of diversification.

c. The company is using the technique of prevention.

d. The warehouse owner is using the technique of reduction.

Educational Objective 2

2-1. Elements necessary to describe a loss exposure include an asset exposed to loss, a cause of loss (also called a peril), and financial consequences of that loss.

2-2. These types of assets could be loss exposures:

    a. An organization's assets could be property, investments, money that is owed to the organization, cash, intangible assets, and human resources.

    b. An individual's assets could be property, investments, money that is owed to the individual, cash, professional qualifications, a unique skill set, and valuable experience.

2-3. Insurers typically define hazards according to these four classifications: (1) moral hazard—a condition that increases the frequency and/or severity of loss resulting from a person acting dishonestly, such as exaggerating a loss; (2) morale hazard—a condition that increases the frequency and/or severity of loss resulting from careless or indifferent behavior, such as failing to lock a vehicle; (3) physical hazard—a condition of property, persons, or operations that increases the frequency and/or severity of loss, such as an icy sidewalk; (4) legal hazard—a condition of the legal environment that increases the frequency or severity of loss, such as the fact that courts in certain districts are more likely to award large liability settlements.

2-4. Three factors that affect the financial consequences of a loss include the type of loss exposure, the cause of loss, and the loss frequency and severity.

2-5. These answers describe types of property:

    a. Tangible property is property that has a physical form, such as a piece of equipment.

    b. Intangible property is property that has no physical form, such as a patent or copyright.

    c. Real property is tangible property consisting of land, all structures permanently attached to the land, and whatever is growing on the land.

    d. Personal property is all tangible property other than real property.

2-6. These answers address financial losses from loss exposures:

    a. A loss can result from damage (including destruction, taking, or loss of use) to property in which the person or organization has a financial interest.

    b. A loss can result from a claim alleging that the person or organization is legally responsible for bodily injury and/or property damage.

    c. A loss can result from a key person's death, disability, retirement, or resignation that deprives an organization of that person's special skill or knowledge.

    d. A loss can result from a reduction in net income, often the result of property, liability, or personnel loss.

2-7. These answers address ABC's hazards:

    a. ABC's employees may intentionally cause a loss or exaggerate a loss that has occurred, thinking that insurance will pay for it.

    b. ABC's employees might drive carelessly, fail to lock an unattended building, or fail to clear an icy sidewalk to protect pedestrians.

c. ABC's employees might increase the likelihood of an accident by failing to correct defects in used cars, putting an excessive number of cars on the lot, or reducing the lighting on the lot.

d. People living in ABC's geographic area might be more litigious than those in other areas, or the local courts might be considered more likely to deliver adverse verdicts or to grant large damage awards in liability suits than those in other areas.

Educational Objective 3

3-1. Named-perils policies provide coverage only for perils that are specifically named in the policy, while direct physical loss policies provide coverage for all perils that are not specifically excluded.

3-2. Business income insurance, also called consequential loss insurance, is designed to provide coverage for the loss of business income and, if necessary, extra expenses incurred while repairs are made after a covered loss. These losses are sometimes referred to as "time element losses" or "business interruption losses."

3-3. One risk builders have is that the value of a building under construction increases as the construction progresses. This requires coverage limits that increase as their project progresses. Another characteristic that requires special consideration is that there are typically several different insured interests involved in a building under construction, such as the building owner, the contractor, and any subcontractors hired. The third characteristic is the additional exposure to a building under construction, such as increased susceptibility to theft because construction materials are left in the open and vulnerability to windstorm or fire in the early stages of construction.

3-4. The concept of legal liability is what distinguishes liability loss exposures from other types of loss exposures. General liability insurance provides coverage when the insured becomes legally obligated to pay damages. An insured may become legally obligated to pay damages as the result of a legal wrong for which the applicable civil law provides a remedy in the form of damages.

3-5. D&O coverage is provided on forms developed by the insurers who write this coverage rather than by a policy form publisher, such as Insurance Services Office, Inc. (ISO). Coverage A, sometimes called "Side A," insures the individual directors and officers. Coverage B, often called "Side B," insures the corporation for the amounts that it is lawfully permitted or required to pay to defend or to settle claims against the directors or officers. These legal costs represent a significant exposure. Some policies also provide entity coverage for the organization in addition to its directors and officers. Almost all D&O policies have a claims-made coverage trigger.

3-6. Three common elements of aviation loss exposures distinguish them from other types of loss exposures:

- The potential for catastrophic loss

- A limited spread of risk

- Diversifying factors that distinguish the loss exposures of each individual aircraft and pilot

3-7. General liability policies exclude liability that is the subject of motor vehicle, workers compensation (employee accident and sickness), and other exposures that are typically covered under other policy types. General liability policies also contain exclusions for most types of environmental liability and many types of cyber risk.

Direct Your Learning ▶▶

4

Operational, Financial, and Strategic Risk

After learning the content of this assignment, you should be able to:

1. Describe operational risk and its subcategories.

2. Explain how risk indicators are used to track the level of operational risk.

3. Describe financial risk and its subcategories.

4. Apply the concepts of value at risk and earnings at risk to financial risk.

5. Explain how regulatory capital provides protection from the downside of financial and operational risks.

6. Apply the concept of economic capital to insurers.

7. Describe strategic risk and its major subcategories.

▶▶

4.1

Outline

▶ **Operational Risk**
   A. Operational Risk in General
   B. Operational Risk Definitions
   C. People, Process, Systems, and External Events
      1. People
      2. Process
      3. Systems
      4. External Events
▶ **Operational Risk Indicators**
   A. Introduction to Risk Indicators
   B. Indicators by Operational Risk Class
   C. Exposure Indicators
   D. Control Indicators
   E. Relating Indicators and Outcomes
▶ **Financial Risk**
   A. Financial Risk in General
   B. Market Risk
      1. Currency Price Risk
      2. Interest Rate Risk
      3. Commodity Price Risk
      4. Equity Price Risk
      5. Liquidity Risk
   C. Credit Risk
   D. Price Risk
▶ **Value at Risk and Earnings at Risk**
   A. Value at Risk
   B. Earnings at Risk
▶ **Regulatory Capital**
   A. Introduction to Regulatory Capital
   B. Regulatory Risk Capital Under Basel II
▶ **Economic Capital**
   A. Fair Value Accounting
   B. Fair Value of Insurers
   C. Economic Capital for Insurers
   D. Advantages and Disadvantages of Economic Capital
      Analysis
   E. Solvency II

▶ **Strategic Risk**
   A. Economic Environment
      1. GDP
      2. Inflation
      3. Financial Crises
      4. International Trade Flows and Restrictions
   B. Demographics
   C. Political Environment

s.m.a.r.t. **tips**   Use the SMART Online Practice Exams to test your understanding of the course material. You can review questions over a single assignment or multiple assignments, or you can take an exam over the entire course.

For each assignment, you should define or describe each of the Key Words and Phrases and answer each of the Review and Application Questions.

Educational Objective 1
Describe operational risk and its subcategories.

Review Questions

1-1. Identify the four categories typically used in an operational risk framework.

1-2. Identify five factors underlying the recent emphasis on operational risk.

1-3. Describe strategies that can be used to mitigate operational risk associated with people.

1-4. Describe the role of an organization's culture in managing operational people risk.

1-5. Summarize process risk and how it can be managed.

1-6. Describe the two types of systems risk.

Application Question

1-7. A multinational organization has a CEO who has been in her role for ten years. The organization's CFO has been in his role for fifteen years. Describe an operational risk for this organization and how it can be managed.

Educational Objective 2
Explain how risk indicators are used to track the level of operational risk.

Key Words and Phrases

Root cause

Key risk indicator (KRI)

Exposure indicator

Loss ratio

Control indicator

Review Questions

2-1. Explain how risk management is applied in the progression of issues to losses.

2-2.   Describe a requirement for key risk indicators (KRIs) to be effective.

2-3.   Identify three risk indicators for the operational risk class of people.

2-4.   Identify three risk indicators for the operational risk class of processes.

2-5.   Identify three risk indicators for the operational risk class of systems.

2-6.   Compare exposure indicators and control indicators.

Application Question

2-7. An organization is experiencing a greater frequency of employee injuries. The risk manager believes this trend may be related to an increase in employee turnover. Explain how the risk manager could evaluate this theory.

Educational Objective 3
Describe financial risk and its subcategories.

Key Words and Phrases

Risk optimization

Hedging

Systematic risk

Interest rate risk

Swap

Cash matching

Zero-coupon bond

Reinvestment risk

Commodity price risk

Cash flow

Commodity futures contract

Equity price risk

Call option

Put option

Price risk

Review Questions

3-1. Identify the two characteristics of financial risk.

3-2. Describe the goal of risk optimization in financial risk management.

3-3. List the major categories of market risk.

3-4. Contrast credit risk with market risk.

3-5. Identify the two types of credit risk.

3-6. Describe the two aspects of price risk.

Application Question

3-7. A manufacturing organization is considering building a factory in another
country. Identify the major financial risks the organization should consider.

Educational Objective 4

Apply the concepts of value at risk and earnings at risk to financial risk.

Key Words and Phrases

Earnings at risk

Conditional value at risk

Monte Carlo simulation

Review Questions

4-1. Explain what value at risk (VaR) measures.

4-2. Identify three key benefits of VaR as a risk measure.

4-3. Identify the limitation of VaR as a risk measure.

4-4. Describe how the VaR limitation can be addressed.

4-5. Explain what earnings at risk (EaR) represents.

4-6. Compare the benefits and limitations of EaR as a risk measure.

Application Questions

4-7. Explain the meaning of a one-day, 5 percent VaR of $500,000.

4-8. If an organization has a one-day, 5 percent VaR of $100,000, explain whether it can determine the amount by which the VaR threshold may be exceeded.

4-9. Explain what is meant when an organization has EaR of $1,000,000 with 95 percent confidence.

Educational Objective 5
Explain how regulatory capital provides protection from the downside of financial and operational risks.

Key Words and Phrases

Capital

Equity capital

Leverage

Review Questions

5-1. Describe risk capital.

5-2. Describe Tier 1 and Tier 2 capital under Basel I.

5-3. Explain how capital adequacy is determined under Basel I.

5-4. Identify the three pillars of Basel II.

5-5. Explain the two approaches under Basel II for measuring a financial institution's credit risk.

5-6. Describe the three approaches for determining the capital charge for a financial institution's operational risk under Basel II.

Application Questions

5-7. A large financial institution has a total risk-based capital ratio of 8 percent and a Tier 1 capital ratio of 3.5 percent. Explain whether this financial institution has adequate capital.

5-8. Explain why critics believe that Basel II may permit too high a level of leverage at large international financial institutions.

Educational Objective 6
Apply the concept of economic capital to insurers.

Key Words and Phrases

Generally accepted accounting principles (GAAP)

Statutory accounting principles (SAP)

Market value surplus

Review Questions

6-1. Explain the difference between economic capital and other types of regulatory capital.

    a. Describe how a firm's economic capital is developed.

    b. Explain how the value at risk (VaR) concept is used to develop a firm's economic capital.

6-2. Contrast fair value accounting with generally accepted accounting principles (GAAP) and statutory accounting principles (SAP).

6-3. Describe the purpose of market value margin in calculating the fair value of an insurer's liabilities.

6-4. Describe the three pillars of Solvency II.

Application Question

6-5. Autumn Assurance Group has assets at fair value of $100 million. The present value of Autumn's liabilities is $85 million. The market value margin is $5 million. What is Autumn's MVS?

a. Using probability models, Autumn determines that its VaR is $8 million. Autumn may be expected to incur $8 million or greater loss of capital at a .5 percent probability over a one-year period. What is Autumn's economic capital?

b. Does Autumn have excess capital or a deficiency in capital?

Educational Objective 7

Describe strategic risk and its major subcategories.

Key Words and Phrases

Tariff

Demographics

Political risk

Review Questions

7-1. Describe Gross Domestic Product (GDP) as an expression of macroeconomic activity.

7-2. Categorize inflation into three distinct types.

7-3. Describe the most serious problem for many organizations during financial crises.

7-4. Compare free trade agreements to tariffs.

7-5. Describe the demographic trend of population aging.

7-6. Compare organizational and operational political risk.

Application Question

7-7. An electronic manufacturing organization is concerned about the demographic trend of an aging population because most of its customers are young. What can the organization do to address this strategic risk?

Answers to Assignment 4 Questions

NOTE: These answers are provided to give students a basic understanding of acceptable types of responses. They often are not the only valid answers and are not intended to provide an exhaustive response to the questions.

Educational Objective 1

1-1. A typical framework includes these risk categories:

- People
- Process
- Systems
- External events

1-2. These are factors underlying the emphasis on operational risk:

- Headline financial services losses/recognition of risk costs
- Other corporate threats
- Advances in technology
- Business complexity
- Global litigiousness
- Increased competition/squeezed margins
- Regulatory developments
- Insurance environment
- E-commerce
- Frequency of natural disasters
- Trends in risk management

1-3. These are strategies to mitigate people risk:

- Recruitment can be used to identify appropriate candidates for hire.
- Selection procedures can mitigate people risk when hiring employees.
- Training and development of employees can help employees perform effectively.
- Performance management can address risks associated with certain employees.
- Incentives can be used to manage risky behaviors and reward desirable behavior.
- Succession planning can help an organization fill key executive positions.

1-4. Each organization should be aware of the significance of its culture in managing its people risk. Some cultures encourage risk taking, while others encourage risk avoidance. Cultures are mainly informal and therefore can be difficult to change. In addition to observation and informal employee feedback, techniques such as employee surveys can be effective in determining important facets of an organization's culture and provide a basis for making changes when necessary.

1-5. Process risk typically includes the procedures and practices organizations use to conduct their business activities. Managing these risks includes a framework of procedures and a mechanism to identify practices that deviate from the procedures.

1-6. Systems risk includes risks associated with technology and equipment. Technology risks include both the equipment used and the software. Equipment failure may present hazard risk as well as risk for an organization's continuing operations.

1-7. This organization has a risk related to its employment of the CEO and CFO. Both of these critical executives have been in their positions for some time. They could develop personal issues that lead to retirement or they could pursue other positions. The loss of a key executive is a major risk for an organization. The organization can manage this risk by developing a succession plan for these key executive positions.

Educational Objective 2

2-1. Issues lead to incidents, which progress to losses. Risk management is most effective when the issues that may lead to losses are identified and managed before a loss occurs. Analysis of historical losses can identify root causes. A more successful approach is to analyze near misses, or incidents, before a loss occurs. The most successful risk management approach is to identify issues before incidents occur.

2-2. KRIs must be leading, rather than lagging, to be effective. If risky issues can be identified before they lead to incidents, and before the incidents lead to losses, then those issues can be either removed or managed.

2-3. These are risk indicators for the operational risk class of people:

- Education
- Experience
- Staffing levels
- Employee surveys
- Customer surveys
- Compensation and experience benchmarked to industry
- Incentives such as bonuses
- Authority levels
- Management experience

2-4. These are risk indicators for the operational risk class of processes:

- Quality scorecards

- Analysis of errors

- Areas of increased activity or volume

- Review of outcomes

- Internal and external review

- Identification of areas of highest risk

- Quality of internal audit procedures

2-5. These are risk indicators for the operational risk class of systems:

- Benchmarks against industry standards

- Internal and external review

- Analysis to determine stress points and weaknesses

- Identification of areas of highest risk

- Testing

- Monitoring

2-6. Exposure indicators are indicators that are integral to an organization's operations. Control indicators usually provide information about an organization's management.

2-7. The risk manager could use a regression to evaluate the trend in employee turnover related to employee injuries over the previous five years. If the regression analysis supports the relationship between turnover and employee injuries, the risk manager could then benchmark the organization's trend against that of similar organizations.

Educational Objective 3

3-1. Financial risk has two characteristics. First, it is an external risk with the potential to affect an organization's objectives. Second, the risk can be reduced through a financial contract, such as a derivative.

3-2. The goal of financial risk management is risk optimization. Risk management professionals should have a perspective that includes both protecting against downside risk and capturing upside risk. Although financial risks are external, internal management's risk appetite and tolerance are key components of each organization's risk optimization process.

3-3. These are the major categories of market risk:

- Currency price risk

- Interest rate risk

- Commodity price risk

- Equity price risk

- Liquidity risk

3-4. Unlike market risk, credit risk has only negative potential. If a borrower pays as agreed, there is no realized risk. If a borrower defaults, the downside of risk is realized.

3-5. There are two types of credit risk: firm-specific risk and systemic credit risk. Firm-specific credit risk is specific to a particular financial institution and is associated with its portfolios of credit transactions.

3-6. Price risk has two aspects for most organizations:

- The price charged for the organization's products or services

- The price of assets purchased or sold by an organization

3-7. The organization should consider currency price risk, commodity price risk, and the price risk of its products. The organization faces both downside and upside risk potential in these categories. The organization could receive either a favorable or unfavorable exchange rate. The prices of commodities purchased in the country of operations could rise or fall, as could distribution costs. The organization may be able to charge a lower price for its products if the move provides reduced production costs.

Educational Objective 4

4-1. VaR measures the probability of the loss in an investment's value exceeding a threshold level. In addition to working within a short time horizon, VaR is typically characterized by low probability.

4-2. VaR provides three key benefits as a risk measure:

- The potential loss associated with an investment decision can be quantified.

- Complex positions are expressed as a single figure.

- Loss is expressed in easily understood monetary terms.

4-3. VaR does not accurately measure the extent to which a loss might exceed the VaR threshold.

4-4. The fact that the VaR does not accurately measure the extent to which a loss might exceed the VaR threshold can be addressed with conditional value at risk (CVaR). CVaR provides the same benefits as VaR and also takes into account the extremely large losses that may occur, usually with low probabilities, in the tail of a value distribution.

4-5. The EaR represents the lower end of projected earnings within a specific confidence, such as 95 percent.

4-6.   EaR is helpful in comparing the likely effects of different risk management strategies on earnings. However, there are limitations, including the complexity of the calculations and a need to understand the relationship of different variables on an organization's results.

4-7.   A one-day, 5 percent VaR of $500,000 means there is a 5 percent probability of losing $500,000 or more over the next day.

4-8.   It is not possible to determine accurately the amount by which the VaR threshold may be exceeded.

4-9.   When EaR are $1,000,000 with 95 percent confidence, the EaR are projected to be $1,000,000 or greater 95 percent of the time and less than $1,000,000 5 percent of the time.

Educational Objective 5

5-1.   Risk capital is the level of capital required to provide a cushion against unexpected loss of economic value at a financial institution. The required risk capital is usually within a confidence interval of 95 percent.

5-2.   Basel I defined bank capital based on two tiers:

- Tier 1—Also referred to as core capital, it is essentially the same as the bank's equity capital.

- Tier 2—Also referred to as supplementary capital, it includes all capital other than core capital, such as gains on investment assets, long-term debt with maturity more than five years, and excess reserves for loan losses. Short-term unsecured debts are not included in the definition of capital.

5-3.   Basel I prescribed a total risk-based capital ratio and a Tier I (core) capital ratio as the level of capital adequacy for banks.

Total risk-based capital ratio = Total capital (Tier 1 + Tier 2) / Risk-adjusted assets

Tier 1 (core) capital ratio = Core capital (Tier 1 / Risk-adjusted assets) ≥ 4%

5-4.   These are the three pillars of Basel II:

- Minimum capital requirements that address risk

- Supervisory review

- Market discipline

5-5.   The Basel II capital framework allows two approaches to measuring a financial institution's credit risk: the standardized approach and the Internal Ratings Based (IRB) approach. The standardized approach uses ratings from international rating agencies to determine an institution's creditworthiness. The Internal Ratings Based Approach (IRBA) allows banks to use their advanced internal risk management systems for calculating regulatory capital.

5-6. There are three approaches under Basel II for determining the capital charge for a financial institution's operational risk:

- The basic indicator approach applies a capital charge of 15 percent of average annual gross income over the previous three years.

- The standardized approach applies factors ranging from 12 to 18 percent of annual revenue on each of eight business lines at the financial institution. The eight business lines are corporate finance, trading and sales, retail banking, commercial banking, payment and settlement, agency services, asset management, and retail brokerage.

- The advanced approach allows authorized financial institutions to use their own models. These models must conform to a regulatory framework. A key aspect of this framework is the Basel definition of operational risk as "the risk of loss resulting from inadequate or failed internal processes, people and systems or from external events." Banks will also be required to include four major factors in quantifying operational risk: internal loss data, external loss data, scenario analysis, and business environment and internal control factors.

5-7. This financial institution does not have adequate capital. The total risk-based capital ratio is at the minimum level of capital adequacy at 8 percent. The Tier 1 (core) capital ratio is below the minimum level of 4 percent.

5-8. Basel II, in the advanced approach to operational risk, allows certain large financial institutions to use their own models to determine risk. These models may not adequately identify risk and result in inadequate capital if an unexpected loss occurs.

Educational Objective 6

6-1. Economic capital differs from other types of regulatory capital because rather than being based on a formula, it is based on the fair (market) values of a firm's assets and liabilities as well as their variability.

   a. Economic capital is developed by modeling the potential variability in market value of a firm's assets and liabilities, taking into consideration all of the firm's risks (market, credit, liquidity, underwriting, operational). These risks are considered together to estimate at the firm level the probabilities of various amounts by which the market value of the firm's liabilities may exceed the market value of its assets over a one-year period.

   b. The probability measures of the market value of a firm's liabilities exceeding the market value of its assets is based on the VaR concept, which uses variability in market values of an asset to estimate the probability of a loss in market value exceeding a threshold level over a given time period.

6-2. Fair value measurement, which can be used with GAAP or SAP, is a method to determine the market value of an asset or a liability. Fair value accounting uses only fair value (actual or estimated market values) for all of an organization's assets or liabilities, unlike GAAP or SAP, which use methods other than fair value to determine the value of certain assets or liabilities, such as acquisition cost, amortized cost, and depreciated cost.

6-3. No readily available market exists for insurers' largest liabilities: loss reserves (including loss adjustment expenses) and unearned premium reserves. These liabilities are generally carried on an insurer's balance sheet as the undiscounted estimate of future payments or earned amounts. However, these reserve estimates are uncertain. Therefore, it is unlikely that an insurer would be able to transfer these reserves to a reinsurer or another party at their present value. The assuming entity would require additional payment for the potential that the reserves prove to be inadequate. This additional payment is the market value margin. Therefore, to calculate the fair value of an insurer's reserves, estimated future amounts are discounted to present value and a market value margin is added.

6-4. Solvency II has three pillars. The first deals with quantitative requirements of capital based on each insurer's specific circumstances. This includes a solvency capital requirement akin to economic capital that would ensure a 99.5 percent probability that the insurer would meet its obligations over the next year. The second pillar sets requirements for insurers' internal risk management process and for the supervision of insurers. The third focuses on reporting, disclosure, and transparency of the risk assessment to the public and regulators.

6-5. MVS = Fair value of assets – (Present value of liabilities + Market value margin)

Autumn's MVS = $100 million – ($85 million + $5 million) = $10 million

   a. Autumn's economic capital is $8 million. The VaR is $8 million at the threshold determined by Autumn.

   b. Autumn's MVS of $10 million is larger than its economic capital of $8 million. Therefore, Autumn has excess capital.

Educational Objective 7

7-1. During periods of economic expansion, there is significant positive GDP growth. In contrast, recessions are characterized by negative GDP growth.

7-2. Mild inflation is within a central bank's target rate. A second category of inflation involves large increases in the rate of inflation. The third category is deflation, which is a decrease in the rate of inflation.

7-3. The most serious problem for many organizations during financial crises is restricted access to credit. Most organizations fund their daily operations through short-term credit. During serious financial crises, credit markets may seize up, including short-term credit facilities.

7-4. Free trade agreements between governments allow products from other nations to enter their respective markets with few barriers or restrictions. Tariffs impose a tax on imports to favor a nation's own producers.

7-5. Population aging results from increasing life expectancy for older members and declining fertility for younger members.

7-6. Organizational risks are risks related to an organization's financial capacity and expertise to operate internationally. Operational political risks are those risks that apply to the countries where an organization operates and include regulations, competitive environment, taxes, and the potential for loss of assets from governmental actions.

7-7. The organization can research and develop products that appeal to an older demographic group. The organization can also target its advertising and promotions toward an older segment of the population. By recognizing the risk that this trend represents, the organization can outpace its competitors by developing new products and adapting existing products.

B

Direct Your Learning ▶▶

Risk Management Framework and Process

Educational Objectives

After learning the content of this assignment, you should be able to:

1. Describe the purpose and component parts of an enterprise risk management framework.

2. Explain how to design and implement an enterprise risk management framework and process.

3. Compare the enterprise-wide risk management process with the traditional risk management process.

4. Apply the enterprise risk management framework and process to an organization's hazard risk.

Outline

▶ **Modeling an Enterprise Risk Management Framework and Process**

A. Purpose of a Risk Management Framework

B. Enterprise Risk Management Framework and Process Model

C. Components of a Risk Management Framework

   1. Lead and Establish Accountability
   2. Align and Integrate
   3. Allocate Resources
   4. Communicate and Report

D. Risk Management Policy

▶ **Designing and Implementing an Enterprise Risk Management Framework and Process**

A. Gap Analysis

B. Evaluation of Internal and External Environments

   1. Internal Environment
   2. External Environment

C. Integration Into Existing Processes

D. Commitment of Resources

E. Communication and Reporting

   1. Communication
   2. Reporting

F. Monitoring and Improvement

▶ **Comparing the Enterprise-Wide Risk Management Process With the Traditional Risk Management Process**

A. Enterprise-Wide Risk Management Process

   1. Scan the Environment
   2. Identify Risks
   3. Analyze Risks
   4. Treat Risks
   5. Monitor and Assure

B. Traditional Risk Management Process

   1. Identifying Loss Exposures
   2. Analyzing Loss Exposures
   3. Examining the Feasibility of Risk Management Techniques
   4. Selecting the Appropriate Risk Management Techniques

5. Implementing the Selected Risk Management Techniques

6. Monitoring Results and Revising the Risk Management Program

C. Similarities

D. Differences

▶ **Applying the Enterprise Risk Management Framework and Process**

A. Case Facts

B. Overview of Steps

C. Applying the Risk Management Framework

   1. Lead and Establish Accountability
   2. Align and Integrate
   3. Allocate Resources
   4. Communicate and Report

D. Applying the Risk Management Process

   1. Scan Environment
   2. Identify Risks
   3. Analyze Risks
   4. Treat Risks
   5. Monitor and Assure

The SMART Online Practice Exams can be tailored to cover specific assignments, so you can focus your studies on topics you want to master.

For each assignment, you should define or describe each of the Key Words and Phrases and answer each of the Review and Application Questions.

Educational Objective 1
Describe the purpose and component parts of an enterprise risk management framework.

Key Words and Phrases

Risk owner

Key performance indicator (KPI)

Key risk indicator (KRI)

Review Questions

1-1. Describe the fundamental purpose of a risk management framework.

1-2. Compare an organization's internal and external environments.

1-3. List the four components of the framework model.

1-4. Identify the techniques an organization can use to establish accountability for risk management.

1-5. Describe the reporting aspect of the enterprise-wide risk management process.

1-6. Explain the importance of a risk management policy statement.

Application Question

1-7. Write a statement of commitment to risk management that your organization could use in its risk management policy. (Answers may vary.)

Educational Objective 2

Explain how to design and implement an enterprise risk management framework and process.

Key Word or Phrase

P-D-C-A Cycle   *Plan Do check Act*

Review Questions

2-1. Explain the purpose and process of a gap analysis in designing and implementing a risk management framework.

2-2. Compare evaluations of an organization's internal and external environments for the risk management framework.

2-3. Describe the two key elements to successful implementation of a risk management framework and process into existing organizational processes.

2-4. List the categories of necessary resources to implement a risk management framework and process.

2-5. Explain the importance of communicating an organization's risk management policy.

2-6. Explain the purpose of the plan-do-check-act (P-D-C-A) cycle in risk management.

Application Question

2-7. Beth's organization has decided to use an enterprise risk management framework. As Beth works on the design of this framework, what should she do to optimize resources?

Educational Objective 3
Compare the enterprise-wide risk management process with the traditional risk management process.

Key Words and Phrases

Risk control

Risk financing techniques

Review Questions

3-1. Identify the five steps of the enterprise-wide risk management process.

3-2. List the major factors used to define risk criteria.

3-3. Identify the six steps of the traditional risk management process.

3-4. Describe how loss exposures are analyzed in the traditional risk management process.

3-5. Describe the major difference between the enterprise-wide risk management process and the traditional risk management process.

Application Question

3-6. An energy organization is considering expanding its pilot operation of converting waste into electricity. The expansion would involve building a generator and then hiring employees to transport waste from a nearby landfill to the generator. Other employees would be hired to supervise and manage the chemical conversion process. The organization would need to issue bonds to pay for this project. Although the organization's pilot has been a success, this is a new energy field with no widespread applications.

Compare the quadrants of risk in this project that would be identified in the enterprise-wide risk management process versus the traditional risk management process.

Educational Objective 4
Apply the enterprise risk management framework and process to an organization's hazard risk.

Application Question

4-1. Sol-Ar is a growing organization that installs solar panels. It is based in a southwestern city in the United States, and its assembly plant employs sixty people. It has six trucks that are used for installation and service, with fifteen technicians and twenty-five assistant technicians employed in the installation and service division.

As Sol-Ar has grown over its five years of existence, its losses have also grown. Employee injuries have increased more than sales. The most frequent and severe injuries are back strains at the plant, but Sol-Ar had one serious injury to a technician who fell from a roof during the installation of a panel. Vehicle accidents have increased in frequency but not severity. One serious liability claim occurred related to a solar panel that fell during installation, injuring a bystander, and several minor liability claims occurred related to property damage from leakage around the panel installation.

Sol-Ar recently decided to hire a risk manager to assist the chief financial officer (CFO) with risk management. Janet has just started in that role.

   a.   Identify Sol-Ar's key hazard risks arising from internal causes, and categorize them according to high or low potential impact and high or low potential likelihood.

   b.   For each of the identified risks, determine whether Janet should recommend risk treatment and, if so, which treatment.

Answers to Assignment 5 Questions

NOTE: These answers are provided to give students a basic understanding of acceptable types of responses. They often are not the only valid answers and are not intended to provide an exhaustive response to the questions.

Educational Objective 1

1-1. The fundamental purpose of a risk management framework is to integrate risk management throughout the organization. The framework is intended to support a risk management process. The principle that underlies a risk management framework is that risk management should add value to the organization. It should not only reduce negative risk but also contribute to profit, reputation, and health and safety.

1-2. The external environment includes the social, political, regulatory, economic, technological, natural, and competitive environments. The internal environment includes organizational structure, objectives, strategies, resources, information systems, and culture.

1-3. These are the four components of the framework model:

- Lead and establish accountability

- Align and integrate

- Allocate resources

- Communicate and report

1-4. These techniques can be used to establish accountability:

- Identify risk owners and their roles in the organization

- Establish key performance indicators (KPI)

- Establish key risk indicators (KRI) and use them to evaluate performance

- Develop risk criteria to evaluate the significance of risks

1-5. The risk management framework should include procedures to report information about risks and the results of risk management to appropriate stakeholders. Senior management should receive executive summary reports at regular intervals. More detailed reports should be prepared and reviewed by managers regarding risks in their areas of responsibility. For the risk management process to be optimally effective, information about emerging risks should be included in risk reports.

1-6. To obtain buy-in from managers and employees throughout the organization, a clear statement of the risk management policy should be present. The policy should support the risk management framework and be communicated throughout the organization and to appropriate external stakeholders.

1-7. "We believe that risk management must be an integral part of all our operations to support our objectives of providing the best value for our customers and shareholders while promoting the safety, health, and well-being of our employees. Risk management should be practiced in all our decisions and activities. Senior management is committed to dedicating the necessary attention and resources to achieving world-class risk management."

Educational Objective 2

2-1. A gap analysis compares an organization's risk management framework and process with an internationally recognized standard, such as ISO 31000 or COSO ERM, thereby allowing the organization to focus resources on addressing any gaps in its framework. By identifying gaps in the organization's risk management program, the analysis helps eliminate the need to redesign existing portions of the standard framework.

2-2. The evaluation of an organization's internal environment provides necessary information about the organization for the risk management framework. It begins with the organization's objectives, risk appetite, and strategies and progresses to risks in different areas of the organization. Communication channels and resources need to be evaluated to determine how to implement the framework effectively. The evaluation of an organization's external environment provides information about the organization's technological capabilities and economic, political, legal and regulatory, natural, and competitive landscapes. Risk management professionals should evaluate the external environment for all of the organization's operations.

2-3. There are two major keys to successful integration of the risk management framework and process. The first is to align risk management objectives and policy with the organization's overall objectives and risk appetite. The second is to use existing processes.

2-4. These are the categories of necessary resources to implement a risk management framework and process:

   • Technology, including equipment and systems

   • Administrative persons

   • Specialists, either internal or external

   • Analysts

   • Training

2-5. Communicating the risk management policy is a key step in integrating the risk management framework and process throughout the organization. The way the policy is communicated sets the tone, and the quality of communications helps ensure the successful integration of the framework and process.

2-6. The P-D-C-A Cycle can be used in many different settings as an improvement model. The "act" step simultaneously restarts the cycle, with evaluation of the implemented improvement reinitiating the "plan" phase.

2-7. To optimize resources while designing her organization's risk management framework, Beth should first conduct a gap analysis to compare her organization's current risk management program with the framework of an international standard selected by the organization. She should carefully analyze and match each element of the enterprise risk management framework to the processes in her organization. She can then optimize resources by focusing on the gaps between the current program and the enterprise risk management framework.

Educational Objective 3

3-1. There are five steps of the enterprise-wide risk management process:

- Scan environment
- Identify risks
- Analyze risks
- Treat risks
- Monitor and assure

3-2. These factors should be considered in defining risk criteria:

- Causes of risk
- Effects of risk
- Metrics used to measure risk effects
- Timeframe of potential effects
- Methods to determine level of risk
- Approach to combinations of risk

3-3. These are the six steps of the traditional risk management process:

- Identifying loss exposures
- Analyzing loss exposures
- Examining feasibility of risk management techniques
- Selecting the appropriate risk management techniques
- Implementing selected risk management techniques
- Monitoring results and monitoring the risk management program

3-4. Loss exposures are analyzed along these four dimensions:

- Loss frequency—the number of losses (such as property damage, liability claims, bad debt charge-offs, or employee thefts) within a specific time period
- Loss severity—the amount, in dollars, of a loss for a specific occurrence
- Total dollar losses—the total dollar amount of losses for all occurrences during a specific time period
- Timing—when losses occur and when loss payments are made

3-5. The most significant difference between the enterprise-wide risk management process and the traditional risk management process is the type of risk addressed.

The traditional risk management process primarily addresses hazard risk along with some operational risk. The traditional approach views risk as having only negative potential for the organization, and the purpose of the risk management process is to minimize the effect of risk.

The enterprise-wide risk management approach addresses all four quadrants of risk—strategic, financial, and operationa,l in addition to hazard risk. This approach views risk as having both negative and positive potential. The purpose of the enterprise-wide risk management process is to optimize the effects of risk on the organization.

3-6. The traditional risk management process would only evaluate the hazard risk associated with the project. This process would identify hazard risks such as risks of employee injuries, damage to the building, or operational risks associated with business interruption. The enterprise-wide risk management process would identify those hazard risks, but also identify financial risks, such as those related to the bond issue, the strategic risk of potential failure in a new process, and operational risks of delivering sufficient electricity to customers if the project is not successful.

Educational Objective 4

4-1. These answers relate to Sol-Ar's risk management process:

a. These are Sol-Ar's key hazard risks arising from internal causes:

- Risk of employee injury at the plant—high likelihood and high impact
- Risk of installation technician injury—low likelihood and high impact
- Vehicle accidents—high likelihood and high impact
- Technician injury related to installation of panels—low likelihood and high impact
- Property damage related to installation of panels—high likelihood and low impact

b.   These are the recommended risk treatments for Sol-Ar's hazard risks:

- Risk of employee injury at the plant—This risk, with high likelihood and high impact, should be treated. A combination of changing the likelihood, changing the impact, and transferring the risk should be used. Janet should analyze what is causing the frequent back strains and explore methods to reduce their likelihood. She should examine claim handling and explore options to reduce the impact of the injuries that do occur. Workers compensation insurance should be used to transfer a portion of this risk.

- Risk of installation technician injury—This risk, with low likelihood and high impact, should be transferred. Because the frequency is low, this risk does not require options to change the likelihood or impact at this time. Workers compensation insurance is usually required and is appropriate to transfer a portion of the risk of a serious injury.

- Vehicle accidents—This risk should be treated by changing the likelihood and impact and transferring a portion of the risk. Although severity has not increased, frequency has, and the potential exists for an accident with serious impact. Janet should explore options to reduce frequency, such as hiring technicians with good driving records and conducting driver-safety training. She should also explore methods to reduce potential impact, such as determining whether technicians are using seat belts. A portion of the vehicle liability risk should be transferred.

- Technician injury related to installation of panels—This risk should be treated by changing the likelihood and transferring a portion of the risk. Although only one serious injury has occurred, the impact of this type of injury is high. Janet should review installation and material-handling procedures to identify options to reduce the likelihood of this type of risk. A portion of this risk should be transferred through liability insurance.

- Property damage related to installation of panels—This risk should be treated. As with the risk of injury from panel installation, Janet should review the installation techniques and identify options to reduce the likelihood of this risk. Sol-Ar may wish to retain a significant portion of this risk, but some of it should be transferred because of the risk of serious property damage.

Direct Your Learning

Risk Identification

Educational Objectives

After learning the content of this assignment, you should be able to:

1. Describe risk identification and its purpose.

2. Explain how an organization can use each of the following team-oriented techniques to identify its risks:
   - Facilitated workshops
   - Delphi technique
   - Scenario analysis
   - HAZOP (hazard and operability study)
   - SWOT (strengths, weaknesses, opportunities, and threats)

3. Describe the purpose and the composition of a risk register.

4. Describe the purpose and the composition of a risk map.

5. Describe the following methods of loss exposure identification:
   - Document analysis
   - Compliance review
   - Personal inspections
   - Expertise within and beyond the organization

6. Given a description of a business operation, recommend techniques for identifying and mapping risk.

Outline

▶ **Introduction to Risk Identification**
  A. Definition of Risk Identification
  B. Risk Identification Tools
  C. Holistic Approach to Risk Identification

▶ **Team Approaches to Risk Identification**
  A. Facilitated Workshops
  B. Delphi Technique
  C. Scenario Analysis
  D. HAZOP
  E. SWOT

▶ **Risk Registers**
  A. Purpose of Risk Registers
  B. Use of Risk Registers With Scenario Models
  C. Organizational Risk Register

▶ **Risk Maps**
  A. Basic Risk Map
  B. Risk Map Variations
  C. Illustrating Risk Treatment Decisions

▶ **Identifying Loss Exposures**
  A. Document Analysis
     1. Risk Assessment Questionnaires and Checklists
     2. Financial Statements and Underlying Accounting Records
     3. Contracts
     4. Insurance Policies
     5. Organizational Policies and Records
     6. Flowcharts and Organizational Charts
     7. Loss Histories
  B. Compliance Review
  C. Personal Inspections
  D. Expertise Within and Beyond the Organization

▶ **Identifying Risk**
  A. Case Facts
  B. Case Analysis Tools
  C. Overview of Steps
  D. Identifying Risks—Team Approach
  E. Risk Register

F. Risk Mapping

s.m.a.r.t. tips

When you take the randomized full practice exams in the SMART Online Practice Exams product, you are seeing the same kinds of questions you will see when you take the actual exam.

For each assignment, you should define or describe each of the Key Words and Phrases and answer each of the Review and Application Questions.

Educational Objective 1
Describe risk identification and its purpose.

Review Questions

1-1. Compare the traditional risk identification process with the process in the ISO 31000 and COSO ERM standards.

1-2. Describe the advantages and the major disadvantage of loss histories as a risk management tool.

1-3. Identify one advantage and one disadvantage of checklists as a risk identification tool.

1-4. Explain why many organizations find it difficult to put a holistic approach to risk identification into practice.

1-5. Describe how risk quadrants can be used to identify risk.

1-6. Compare the top-down and bottom-up approaches to risk identification.

Application Question

1-7. The new chief risk officer (CRO) at an organization is interested in identifying emerging risks. The organization was recently surprised by a lawsuit regarding a defect in one of its products. What method should the risk manager recommend to the CRO to identify emerging risks at the organization?

Educational Objective 2

Explain how an organization can use each of the following team-oriented techniques to identify its risks:

- **Facilitated workshops**
- **Delphi technique**
- **Scenario analysis**
- **HAZOP (hazard and operability study)**
- **SWOT (strengths, weaknesses, opportunities, and threats)**

Review Questions

2-1. Explain why it is helpful to include representatives from diverse groups in an organization during team workshops to identify risks.

2-2. Describe the Delphi technique.

2-3. Compare the advantages and disadvantages of scenario analysis in identifying risks. A company receives an annuity payment of $15,000 each year for three years at a discount rate of 3 percent.

2-4. Identify the steps in a hazard and operability study, or HAZOP, approach to risk identification.

2-5. Describe the SWOT approach to risk identification.

2-6. Explain the ideal outcome of a strengths, weaknesses, opportunities, and threats (SWOT) analysis.

Application Question

2-7. Initial Corp. designs software for marketing and customer service applications. It has dropped from double-digit to single-digit growth over the previous three years. One of its customers introduced Initial's owner to the owner of RiskMap, which designs risk management software. RiskMap's owner would like to retire but is the company's lead designer; also on staff are two programmers who have been with the company since its inception ten years ago. RiskMap's business has grown every year, with an average growth of 20 percent. Initial Corp. is considering acquiring RiskMap.

a. Perform a strengths, weaknesses, opportunities, and threats (SWOT) analysis of Initial Corp.'s potential acquisition of RiskMap.

b. Explain your concluding recommendation regarding this potential acquisition.

Educational Objective 3
Describe the purpose and the composition of a risk register.

Key Word or Phrase
Risk register

Review Questions
3-1. Describe the purpose of a risk register.

3-2. List some of the advantages of a computerized risk register.

3-3. Explain how the level of risk is determined on the risk register.

3-4. Describe the use of scenario models to create an organization risk register.

3-5. Explain how color coding can be used in risk registers.

3-6. Identify the characteristics a risk register should have.

Application Question

3-7.   An organization manufactures chemicals at one facility in the United States. Develop a risk register for a fire risk scenario for this organization and identify risks in all four risk quadrants.

Educational Objective 4
Describe the purpose and the composition of a risk map.

Key Words and Phrases

Risk map

Optimum risk

Review Questions

4-1.   Describe the purpose of a basic risk map.

4-2.   Explain the use of different colors in a risk map.

4-3.   Explain how a time dimension can be added to a risk map.

4-4.   Describe the importance of inherent and residual risk.

4-5.   Compare residual risk with optimum risk.

4-6.   Describe how a risk map can be used to analyze risk treatment.

Application Question

4-7.   Matt is the risk manager for a well-known jeweler. The jeweler has retail stores in New York, Los Angeles, Paris, and London. It has recently started selling jewelry worldwide over the Internet. Matt assembled a team to identify the key risks associated with the new Internet operations. The team identified these key risks: data breach of customer credit information, employee injuries at the New York international distribution center, employee theft, exchange rate risk, delivery delays, and peak production demands during holidays. Design a risk map that prioritizes these risks.

Educational Objective 5

Describe the following methods of loss exposure identification:

- **Document analysis**
- **Compliance review**
- **Personal inspections**
- **Expertise within and beyond the organization**

Key Words and Phrases

Balance sheet

Income statement

Statement of cash flows

Hold-harmless agreement (or indemnity agreement)

Indemnification

Hazard analysis

Review Questions

5-1. Identify the types of internal and external documents an organization may use to analyze loss exposures.

5-2. Describe an advantage and a disadvantage of using questionnaires in assessing loss exposures.

5-3. Describe how an organization uses these documents to identify loss exposures.

   a.   Financial statements

b. Contracts

c. Insurance policies

d. Organizational policies and records

e. Flowcharts and organizational charts

f. Loss histories

5-4. Describe how a compliance review may facilitate the identification of loss exposures.

Educational Objective 6

Given a description of a business operation, recommend techniques for identifying and mapping risk.

Application Question

6-1. Laura is the risk manager at Pharmacy, Inc., a national chain of retail pharmacies. She is working on a project assigned by the chief risk officer (CRO) and the chief executive officer (CEO) to identify Pharmacy's risks. The CRO wants to develop a holistic approach to Pharmacy's risks. Both the CRO and CEO want to identify as many of Pharmacy's risks and their potential effects on the organization as possible.

a. Explain whether you would recommend that Laura use a team approach to risk identification and, if so, which one.

b. Design a risk register that Laura and her team can use for Pharmacy's risks.

c.   A level-ten risk on a scale from one to ten, with ten being the highest level, is identified as the risk that a pharmacist fills a prescription incorrectly, resulting in serious injury to a customer. Populate your risk register for this risk.

Answers to Assignment 6 Questions

NOTE: These answers are provided to give students a basic understanding of acceptable types of responses. They often are not the only valid answers and are not intended to provide an exhaustive response to the questions.

Educational Objective 1

1-1. The traditional risk identification process involves identifying loss exposures, which are negative risks. Standards such as ISO 31000 and COSO ERM use a broader approach in identifying risks with positive as well as negative potential for the organization.

1-2. Loss histories offer several advantages. They provide quantitative and qualitative information regarding known risks. They usually are contained within a database that can be adapted to various types of analysis. Loss histories can also be correlated with their effect on the organization's objectives. However, a disadvantage of loss histories is that they are lagging rather than leading indicators of risk.

1-3. An advantage of checklists is their ease of use by non-risk-management professionals. A disadvantage of checklists is the possibility of failing to identify key risks or not identifying the effects of risks on other areas of the organization.

1-4. For most organizations, different types of risks are concentrated in specific areas. This silo nature of risk can prevent or delay risk identification and an understanding of how risk may ripple through an organization.

1-5. The use of risk quadrants to identify and categorize risk can provide a framework for holistic risk identification. After the risks have been identified in each quadrant, a scenario analysis can be performed to assign event likelihoods and consequences. Developed scenarios can represent different levels of severity.

1-6. In a top-down approach, senior management decides which risks pose a significant threat or opportunity for the organization. Although this approach offers a high-level view of the risks that are central to meeting the organization's objectives, it provides a limited view of risks that may be percolating in various areas of the organization.

   In a bottom-up approach, the views of employees are included in identifying risks. However, this approach may take too much time and provide too many details.

1-7. The risk manager should recommend a bottom-up approach to risk identification. The surprise lawsuit indicates that risks may be percolating in one or more areas of the organization. Inspections of manufacturing areas and interviews of employees would assist in identifying risks.

Educational Objective 2

2-1. It is helpful to include representatives from diverse groups in an organization during team workshops because discussion of the combined and cascading effects of risks provides valuable information on risk level and priority. Such discussion can identify opportunity risks as well as risks with potentially negative consequences.

2-2. The Delphi technique uses the opinions of a select group of experts to identify risks. Typically, these experts do not meet but respond to a survey or an inquiry.

2-3. Scenario analysis is useful in identifying a range of potential consequences and in prioritizing risks. An internal cross-functional team at an organization can implement the technique to obtain a multidimensional view of the potential consequences of a risk. Disadvantages to scenario analysis include possibly missing key risks and limited imagination of the team conducting the analysis. Although cross-functional teams reduce these disadvantages, they do not eliminate them.

2-4. With a HAZOP approach to risk identification, a study team assembles in a facilitated workshop and follows these steps:

- Subdivides the project or system design into small components

- Reviews each component to identify risks

- Identifies cause and potential outcome for each risk

- Develops a solution for each risk

2-5. SWOT—an acronym for strengths, weaknesses, opportunities, and threats—is a type of team approach that is useful in analyzing a new project or product. The strengths and weaknesses are internal factors to be considered. The opportunities and threats are external factors.

2-6. The SWOT analysis should ideally conclude with a "Go" or "No Go" recommendation for a specific project and should include discussion on whether weaknesses or threats can be converted into strengths or opportunities.

2-7. These answers relate to Initial Corp.'s potential acquisition of RiskMap:

a. This is a SWOT analysis of the potential RiskMap acquisition:

Strengths	Weaknesses
RiskMap has been growing successfully.	Initial has no experience in risk management software.
An Initial customer introduced the idea, representing potential synergy.	RiskMap's lead designer is the owner and wants to retire.
RiskMap has two experienced programmers.	

Opportunities	Threats
RiskMap has strong, positive growth.	Initial may not be able to replicate RiskMap's success.
RiskMap's growth could offset Initial's slowing growth.	Competitors could attract RiskMap's programmers.
RiskMap represents an opportunity for Initial to diversify.	

b. The recommendation is a "Go." Initial's growth is declining, and it can benefit from RiskMap's strong growth. The introduction of Initial to RiskMap came through one of Initial's customers, indicating that Initial could increase its value to customers through the acquisition, which also presents an opportunity for Initial to diversify.

Although the lead designer at RiskMap is the owner and wants to retire, Initial's designers could likely step in and expand their roles. Additionally, RiskMap's two experienced programmers could conceivably stay with Initial after the acquisition. All points considered, the strengths and opportunities outweigh the weaknesses and threats.

Educational Objective 3

3-1. A risk register provides a matrix to identify risks according to their likelihood and potential consequences for the organization.

3-2. An interactive computer system allows risk owners, such as department managers and project managers, to continually update risk information. Such a system also allows risk management professionals to continually evaluate the information.

3-3. The level of risk indicated in the risk register is determined by the significance to the organization, not merely by multiplying likelihood by consequences (impacts).

3-4. Risk registers can be used to depict all of the organization's risk scenarios. Also, specific scenario risk registers can be combined into one risk register for the entire organization.

3-5. Color codes can be used to highlight the level of risk. Potentially severe and moderate risks could be highlighted in different colors.

3-6. Risk management professionals should ensure the risk register has these characteristics:

- Adequately identifies the organization's risks
- Prioritizes risk according to the potential effect on the organization
- Provides interactive use for risk owners
- Forms a matrix to manage risks

3-7. This is an example of a risk register that identifies risks in all four quadrants for the fire risk scenario of a chemical manufacturing organization:

Scenario	Risk Description	Likelihood	Consequences	Level of Risk	Improvement Action	Review Date
Fire	Fire: minimal to catastrophic	25	$0-$100M+	10	Develop catastrophe plan	3/1/20X3
					Review insurance	1/1/20X3
					Review fire prevention	1/1/20X3
Risk Quadrant	Fire damage	100	$0-$10M	5	Safety procedures	1/1/20X3
Hazard Risks	Employee injuries	50	$0-$1M	10	Safety plan for employees	
Operational Risks	Disruption of production	100	$0-$10M	10	Develop contingency plan	3/1/20X3
	Loss of business records	60	$0-$25K	2	Review business interruption coverage	1/1/20X3
	Period of repair/ rebuilding	100	$0-$10M	9		
Financial Risks	Loss of income	100	$0-$10M	10	Develop contingency plan	5/1/20X3
	Negative effect on share price	70	$0-$5M	8		
Strategic Risks	Reputational damage if injuries or disruption in supplies to customers	25	Potentially major damage	7	Develop contingency plan	3/1/20X3

Measurement Scales:

Likelihood:	1 – 100, 1 = lowest
Level of Risk:	1 – 10, 1 = lowest
Consequences:	Estimated dollar range for quantitative measures List of types of consequences

Educational Objective 4

4-1. A basic risk map provides a matrix of the likelihood and impact (consequences) of risks identified on an organization's risk register.

4-2. Different colors are used to represent different levels of risk, such as the difference in combinations of impact and likelihood. This technique is sometimes referred to as heat mapping.

4-3. Time dimension risk maps can be used with the basic risk map to set priorities for the urgency of risk management. Time dimension risk maps can be used to set monthly, quarterly, or annual priorities.

4-4. The difference between inherent risk, the risk to an entity apart from any action to alter either the likelihood or impact of the risk, and residual risk, the risk remaining after actions to alter the risk's likelihood or impact, provides a measure of the necessity and the effectiveness of the current risk treatment.

4-5. The difference between the residual (current) level of risk and the optimum risk, the level of risk that is within an organization's risk appetite, represents the risk treatment opportunity to further reduce the risk.

4-6. A risk map can be used to depict the effects of an organization's current risk treatment techniques on the likelihood and impact of risks. It can also show opportunities to improve risk treatment.

4-7. This risk map prioritizes the risks identified for the jeweler's Internet operations:

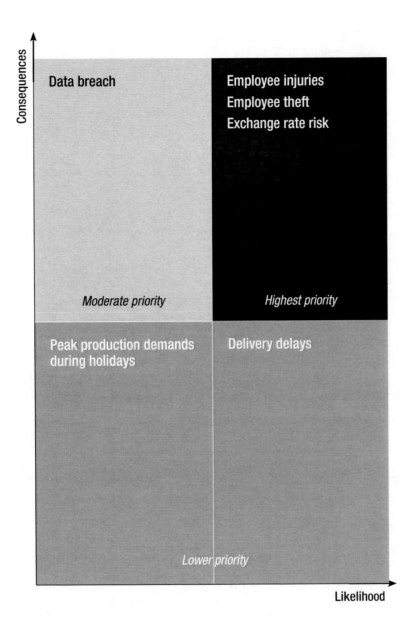

Educational Objective 5

5-1. An organization may use the following types of internal and external documents to analyze loss exposures:

- Internal documents—financial statements, accounting records, contracts, insurance policies, policy and procedure manuals, flowcharts and organizational charts, and loss histories

- External documents—questionnaires, checklists, surveys, Web sites, news releases, and reports from external organizations

5-2. The advantage of questionnaires in assessing loss exposures is that they capture more descriptive information than checklists about amounts or values exposed to loss. Their disadvantage is that they typically require considerable expense, time, and effort to complete and may still not identify all loss exposures.

5-3. These answers describe how an organization uses documents:

a. Balance sheets, income statements, statement of cash flows, and supporting statements help identify major categories of current and past loss exposures and can be used to identify future plans that could lead to new loss exposures. For example, asset entries on a balance sheet indicate property values that could by reduced by loss.

b. Contracts can help identify property and liability loss exposures assumed or transferred by contract and help determine who has assumed responsibility for which loss exposure.

c. Insurance policies can reveal many of the organization's insurable loss exposures.

d. Corporate by-laws, board minutes, employee manuals, procedure manuals, mission statements, and risk management policies may identify existing loss exposures and indicate impending changes that may create new loss exposures.

e. Flowcharts show the nature and use of resources involved in an organization's operations and the sequence of and relationships between the operations. They may also reveal bottlenecks where losses could have substantial effects on business operations. An organizational chart helps identify key personnel for whom the organization may have a personnel loss exposure.

f. An organization's loss history, or that of a comparable organization, can indicate current or future loss exposures.

5-4. Compliance review determines an organization's compliance with local, state, and federal statutes and regulations and can therefore help the organization minimize or avoid liability loss exposures associated with noncompliance.

Educational Objective 6

6-1. These answers relate to identification of Pharmacy, Inc.'s risks:

a. A team approach would be beneficial to Laura. Because the CRO and CEO want a holistic, comprehensive approach to Pharmacy's risks, it will be important for Laura to receive input from all areas of the organization. A facilitated workshop approach would be a helpful technique to identify as many risks as possible and their effects on all areas of the organization.

b.

Risk Description	Strategic	Hazard	Operational	Financial	Level of Risk	Action Plan

c.

Risk Description	Strategic	Hazard	Operational	Financial	Level of Risk	Action Plan
Pharmacist incorrectly fills prescription	Reputational damage	Lawsuit	Review of operations and procedures	Negative effect on share price	10	Review pharmacist hiring and training practices Review quality controls Review casualty insurance

Direct Your Learning

7

Risk Analysis

Educational Objectives

After learning the content of this assignment, you should be able to:

1. Describe risk analysis and its importance.

2. Explain how probability analysis can be used to estimate the likelihood and consequences of an event.

3. Describe the following characteristics of probability distributions:
   - Expected value
   - Mean
   - Standard deviation
   - Coefficient of variation
   - Normal distribution

4. Explain how regression analysis can be used to forecast gains or losses.

5. Compare decision tree analysis and event tree analysis in terms of the methods they use to evaluate event consequences.

6. Explain how to analyze loss exposures considering the four dimensions of loss and data credibility.

Outline

▶ **Introduction to Risk Analysis**
  A. The Nature of Risk Analysis
  B. Qualitative Assessment and Quantitative Analysis
  C. Assessing Controls
▶ **Probability Analysis**
  A. The Nature of Probability
     1. Theoretical and Empirical Probabilities
     2. Law of Large Numbers
  B. Probability Distributions
▶ **Characteristics of Probability Distributions**
  A. Expected Value
  B. Mean
  C. Standard Deviation
  D. Coefficient of Variation
  E. Normal Distribution
  F. Practical Application: Normal Distribution
▶ **Trend Analysis**
  A. Regression Analysis
  B. Regression Analysis Example
▶ **Analyzing Event Consequences**
  A. Decision Tree Analysis
  B. Event Tree Analysis
  C. Comparing Decision Tree Analysis and Event Tree Analysis
▶ **Analyzing Loss Exposures**
  A. Loss Frequency
  B. Loss Severity
     1. Maximum Possible Loss
     2. Frequency and Severity Considered Jointly
  C. Total Dollar Losses
  D. Timing
  E. Data Credibility

Repetition helps students learn. Read, write, and repeat key points for each assignment.

For each assignment, you should define or describe each of the Key Words and Phrases and answer each of the Review and Application Questions.

Educational Objective 1
Describe risk analysis and its importance.

Review Questions

1-1. Contrast qualitative assessment and qualitative analysis.

1-2. Explain how an organization can estimate risk probabilities in the absence of historical data.

1-3. Describe what an organization should verify when assessing controls.

Educational Objective 2
Explain how probability analysis can be used to estimate the likelihood and consequences of an event.

Key Words and Phrases
Theoretical probability

Empirical probability (a posteriori probability)

Probability analysis

Probability distribution

Review Questions

2-1. Contrast theoretical probability and empirical probability.

2-2. The law of large numbers can be used to more accurately forecast future events only when the events being forecast meet three criteria. Identify those criteria.

2-3. Identify the two qualities shared by all outcomes of properly constructed probability distributions.

2-4. Contrast discrete probability distributions and continuous probability distributions.

2-5. Explain how a continuous distribution can be designed to calculate the probability that an outcome will fall within a certain range.

Application Question

2-6. Gibson Manufacturing uses three machines in the manufacture of its products; all machines are regularly maintained. Machines A and B are five years old. Gibson has just purchased the new, improved version of Machine C. One of Machine B's operators has just retired, and a new employee will receive training in operating the machine. The operators of the other machines have all been employed for more than five years. Gibson's risk manager wants to predict the frequency of accidents involving all three machines. Explain how the law of large numbers applies to each of the three machines.

Educational Objective 3

Describe the following characteristics of probability distributions:

- **Expected value**
- **Mean**
- **Standard deviation**
- **Coefficient of variation**
- **Normal distribution**

Key Words and Phrases

Central tendency

Dispersion

Expected value

Mean

Standard deviation

Coefficient of variation

Normal distribution

Review Questions

3-1. Contrast central tendency and dispersion in relation to probability distributions.

3-2. Contrast expected value and mean in relation to probability distributions.

3-3. Contrast standard deviation and coefficient of variation.

3-4. State the percentage value for each of these categories of outcomes in a normal distribution:

a.   Outcomes within one standard deviation above the mean

b.   Outcomes within one standard deviation above and below the mean

c.   Outcomes between one and two standard deviations above the mean

d.   Outcomes in the area between the mean and two standard deviations below the mean

Application Question

3-5.   Reggie is a bicycle courier in a metropolitan area. One of his regular customers requires prompt delivery of paper documents to another business across town. The customer usually notifies Reggie two hours before a document packet will be ready. Reggie estimates his mean commute time from his home to his customer's office is thirty minutes with a standard deviation of ten minutes, depending on traffic and weather conditions. Reggie typically leaves an hour before the designated pick-up time to ensure he is there when the documents are ready; however, he often arrives early and must wait for the documents, losing time during which he could be making other deliveries. Reggie wants to reduce his wait time and still ensure that he is on time. Determine how much time Reggie should allow for his commute, and explain your answer.

Educational Objective 4
Explain how regression analysis can be used to forecast gains or losses.

Key Words and Phrases

Trend analysis

Regression analysis

Linear regression analysis

Review Questions

4-1.   Explain why a risk management professional might use trend analysis.

4-2.   Identify the assumption on which regression analysis is based.

4-3.   Describe two aspects important to the interpretation of linear regressions.

Application Question

4-4. Michael, the risk manager for Charles Construction wants to project the number of employee injuries at construction sites based on its annual income (adjusted for inflation) for the past five years. Michael has constructed a linear regression line and calculated the values of *a* and *b*. The value for *a* indicates that 3.4 injuries occurred for each $100,000 of income, and the value for *b*, 0.042, indicates that an additional injury can be expected with each additional $2,380,095 ($100,000 in income × [1 ÷ 0.042]). Assuming Charles Construction expects $15 million in income next year, calculate its expected number of construction-site injuries for the year.

Educational Objective 5

Compare decision tree analysis and event tree analysis in terms of the methods they use to evaluate event consequences.

Review Questions

5-1. Contrast decision tree analysis with event tree analysis.

5-2. Describe how a decision tree is constructed.

5-3. Describe how an event tree is constructed.

Application Question

5-4. The risk manager for Shelton Manufacturing is concerned about the risk of explosion and fire during one stage of the manufacturing process. Shelton has installed a sprinkler system and fire alarm in the area where explosions are likely. Should an explosion occur that starts a fire, the sprinkler is designed to activate immediately. The heat-activated fire alarm would be triggered by spreading fire.

Describe a process that can be used to estimate the potential effectiveness risk control measures in the event of an explosion.

Educational Objective 6
Explain how to analyze loss exposures considering the four dimensions of loss and data credibility.

Review Questions

6-1. List four dimensions used in the analysis of a loss exposure.

6-2. List the four categories of loss frequency and the three categories of loss severity used in the Prouty Approach.

6-3. List the three categories of loss severity used in the Prouty Approach.

6-4. Describe two approaches a risk management professional may use when jointly analyzing the frequency and loss severity of a loss exposure.

6-5. Explain why timing is an important consideration when analyzing loss exposures.

6-6. Describe the dilemma that insurance and risk management professionals can have when evaluating data credibility.

Answers to Assignment 7 Questions

NOTE: These answers are provided to give students a basic understanding of acceptable types of responses. They often are not the only valid answers and are not intended to provide an exhaustive response to the questions.

Educational Objective 1

1-1. Qualitative assessment measures a risk by the significance of consequences; it may use such ratings as "high," "medium," and "low." Quantitative analysis assigns specific values to consequences and their probabilities to reach a numeric indication of the level of risk.

1-2. In the absence of historical data, an organization may base probability estimations on predictions or expert opinions. Predictive techniques, such as decision tree analysis and event tree analysis, assign numerical values to various components related to a risk and combine them to produce a probability estimate.

1-3. An organization should verify whether each control measure is capable of achieving the intended level of treatment or control and whether its effectiveness can be demonstrated when required. Verification depends on the existence of records and documentation of the control's performance in relation to the risk.

Educational Objective 2

2-1. Theoretical probability is based on theoretical principles rather than on experience. Theoretical probabilities are constant as long as the physical conditions that generate them remain unchanged. Empirical probability is based on actual experience through historical data. Empirical probabilities are only estimates. Their accuracy depends on the size and representative nature of the samples being studied.

2-2. The law of large numbers can be used to more accurately forecast future events only when the events being forecast meet these criteria:

- The events have occurred in the past under substantially identical conditions and have resulted from unchanging, basic causal forces.

- The events can be expected to occur in the future under the same, unchanging conditions.

- The events have been, and will continue to be, both independent of one another and sufficiently numerous.

2-3. A properly constructed probability distribution always contains outcomes that are both mutually exclusive and collectively exhaustive.

2-4. Discrete probability distributions have a finite number of possible outcomes, whereas continuous probability distributions have an infinite number of possible outcomes.

2-5. A continuous distribution can be divided into a finite number of bins to calculate the probability of an outcome falling within a certain range.

2-6. The law of large numbers produces the most accurate predictions under unchanging conditions. Therefore, in the Gibson Manufacturing scenario, the most accurate predictions can be made for Machine A because Gibson has five years of loss experience with the same machine and the same operators. The fact that Machine B will have a new, inexperienced operator is a change of conditions that could make loss forecasts less accurate for that machine. Gibson has no data on which to base the loss experience for the new, improved Machine C.

Educational Objective 3

3-1. Central tendency represents the best guess as to what a probability distribution outcome will be based on a concentration of possible outcomes. Dispersion describes the extent to which a distribution is spread out.

3-2. Expected value measures central tendency by weighting and averaging outcomes. The weights are the probabilities of outcomes. The procedure for calculating the expected value applies to all theoretical discrete probability distributions.

   In an empirical distribution constructed from historical data, the expected value is estimated using the mean. The mean is calculated by weighting each outcome by the relative frequency with which it occurs and dividing by the number of outcome values.

3-3. Both standard deviation and coefficient of variation are measures of dispersion. Standard deviation indicates how widely dispersed the values in a distribution are. Coefficient of variation indicates a distribution's variability relative to its mean or expected value.

3-4. These are the percentages for the selected outcomes in a normal distribution:

   a. Within one standard deviation above the mean—34.13 percent

   b. Within one standard deviation above and below the mean—68.26 percent

   c. Between one and two standard deviations above the mean—13.59 percent

   d. Between the mean and two standard deviations below the mean—47.72 percent

3-5. Based on a normal distribution, Reggie can expect his commute time to be between twenty and forty minutes 68 percent of the time (the thirty-minute mean plus or minus one standard deviation of ten minutes). Commute time will be between ten and twenty minutes 13.59 percent of the time and will be between forty and fifty minutes 13.59 percent of the time. A commute of fifty minutes or more (two standard deviations above the mean) has approximately a 2.28 percent chance of occurring. If Reggie is comfortable with that percentage, he can reduce his commute time by ten minutes.

Educational Objective 4

4-1. A risk management professional might use trend analysis to increase the accuracy of forecasting by examining variables that affect trends. For example, changes in hazard loss frequency or severity might coincide with changes in some other variable, such as production, in a way that allows loss frequency or severity to be forecast more accurately. Trend analysis and regression analysis can also be used to detect and forecast patterns of gains.

4-2. Regression analysis assumes that the variable being forecast varies predictably with another variable.

4-3.   These are two aspects of interpreting linear regressions:

  • A linear regression line might not be accurate when it gets very far away from the actual data values used.

  • The dependent variable's value calculated by the linear regression is not likely to exactly equal the historical value for that past year.

4-4.   The equation for calculating the number of injuries Charles Construction should expect is $y = bx + a$, or y (injuries) = (0.042 × 150 [$15 million stated in $100,000s]) + 3.4 = 9.7. Therefore, the company should expect ten injuries next year.

Educational Objective 5

5-1.   Decision tree analysis examines the consequences, including costs and gains, of decisions. An organization may use decision tree analysis to compare alternative decisions and select the most effective strategy to achieve a goal.

  Event tree analysis examines all possible consequences of an accidental event, their probabilities, and existing measures to prevent or control them. An organization may use this approach to examine the effectiveness of systems, risk treatment, or risk control measures and to identify, recommend, and justify expenditures of money, time, or resources for improvements.

5-2.   Constructing a decision tree begins with a statement of the initial decision under consideration. Various sequences of events ("pathways") are charted for each alternative; each pathway leads to an outcome. For a quantitative analysis, probabilities are assigned to each event on a pathway, and expected values (costs or gains) of each pathway can be estimated for the outcome. The product of the probabilities of each event in a pathway and the value of its outcome can be compared to determine the pathway that produces the highest expected value.

5-3.   The starting point of an event tree is identification of an accidental event. The various progressions of events that could follow the accidental event are then determined, resulting in a list of potential consequences of the initial event and identification of any existing barriers for each consequence. From that information, an event tree diagram is constructed. Barriers are listed in the sequence in which they would be activated should the designated event occur. In each pathway, every barrier has the potential to either function or fail; therefore, the pathway splits in two, and an estimated probability—determined by experts or other analysis—is assigned to both potentials.

  For each pathway in the diagram, the probability is that all its events will occur. The frequency of the consequence of each pathway is the product of the probabilities in the pathway and the frequency of the initial event. The sum of the probabilities of the outcomes, given that the initial event occurs, should total one.

5-4. Event tree analysis can be used to estimate the frequency of success of the Shelton Manufacturing's explosion risk control measures. The event tree would show explosion as the initiating event and would split into two pathways (true and false) indicating whether a fire would result from the explosion. The "true" branch (explosion causes fire) would split again, forming pathways indicating whether the sprinkler system would function or fail, and each of these pathways would split again to indicate whether the alarm system would function or fail. An estimated probability—determined by experts or other analysis—would be assigned to each potential occurrence. The frequency of the consequence of each pathway could be calculated by multiplying the probabilities in the pathway by the frequency of the initial event. The sum of the probabilities of the outcomes, given that an explosion occurs, should total one, and the sum of the outcome frequencies should equal the frequency of explosion.

Educational Objective 6

6-1. These are the four dimensions used in the analysis of a loss exposure:

- Loss frequency—number of losses that occur within a specific period

- Loss severity—dollar amount of loss for a specific occurrence

- Total dollar losses—total dollar amount of losses for all occurrences during a specific period

- Timing—when losses occur and when loss payments are made

6-2. These are the four categories of loss frequency used in the Prouty Approach:

- Almost nil

- Slight

- Moderate

- Definite

6-3. These are the three categories of loss severity used in the Prouty Approach:

- Slight

- Significant

- Severe

6-4. Risk management professionals may use two approaches when jointly analyzing the frequency and loss severity of a loss exposure:

- Prouty Approach—identifies four categories of loss frequency and three categories of loss severity

- Total claims distribution—created by combining the frequency and severity distributions

6-5. Timing is important to consider when analyzing loss exposures because of the time value of money. Money held in reserve can earn interest until the payment is made. In addition, when a loss is counted affects accounting and tax treatment.

6-6. Insurance and risk management professionals can be left with a dilemma answering whether it is better to use older data, which are accurate but may have been generated in an environment that is substantially different from the that of the period for which they are trying to predict, or to use more recent data and sacrifice some accuracy to maintain the integrity of the environment.

Direct Your Learning

Risk Treatment

Educational Objectives

After learning the content of this assignment, you should be able to:

1. Describe the risk treatment process and risk treatment techniques.
2. Describe risk financing and its importance to organizations.

Outline

▶ **Risk Treatment**

   A. Risk Treatment Process

   B. Risk Treatment Techniques

▶ **Introduction to Risk Financing**

   A. Risk Financing as a Part of Risk Treatment

   B. Risk Transfer

      1. Insurance

      2. Contract (Noninsurance)

      3. Hedging

   C. Risk Retention

      1. Planned or Unplanned

      2. Complete or Partial

      3. Funded or Unfunded

Narrow the focus of what you need to learn. Remember, the Educational Objectives are the foundation of the course, and the exam is based on these Educational Objectives.

For each assignment, you should define or describe each of the Key Words and Phrases and answer each of the Review and Application Questions.

Educational Objective 1
Describe the risk treatment process and risk treatment techniques.

Key Words and Phrases

Loss prevention

Loss reduction

Retention

Review Questions

1-1. Describe the goal of risk treatment.

1-2. Explain why it is important to monitor risk treatment plans.

1-3. List the general categories of risk treatment options.

1-4. Describe risk treatment techniques for events that appear to have primarily positive potential outcomes.

Educational Objective 2
Describe risk financing and its importance to organizations.

Key Words and Phrases
Risk financing

Transfer

Risk

Futures contract

Review Questions

2-1. Describe the two categories of risk financing techniques.

2-2. Describe what risk transfer shifts to another party through insurance and noninsurance techniques.

2-3. Explain when hedging is practical.

Application Question

2-4. John is a risk management professional for his employer. His employer's management is trying to decide whether to retain some of the financial consequences of general liability events or transfer them to an insurer. What advantages of transferring the financial consequences of general liability events to an insurer might John point out to management?

Answers to Assignment 8 Questions

NOTE: These answers are provided to give students a basic understanding of acceptable types of responses. They often are not the only valid answers and are not intended to provide an exhaustive response to the questions.

Educational Objective 1

1-1. The goal of risk treatment is to modify identified risks to assist the organization in meeting its objectives.

1-2. Review of risk treatment plans is important because risks may change based on the organization's operation or on environmental factors, such as economic conditions or legal and regulatory requirements. Previous risk treatment decisions may no longer be valid, and implemented controls may no longer be effective. Furthermore, emerging risks such as those arising from new technology or the acquisition of a new business unit must be identified and assessed, and a cost-benefit analysis should be conducted to assess whether the benefits of the chosen treatment option continue to outweigh related costs.

1-3. In general, available risk treatment options fall into the categories of avoidance, modification, transfer, retention, or exploitation.

1-4. For events that appear to have primarily positive potential outcomes, risk treatment techniques would focus on exploiting the risk by maximizing expected gains. Techniques would include modifying the likelihood of an event to increase the opportunity to meet objectives while also considering treatment options for potential negative outcomes.

Educational Objective 2

2-1. Risk financing techniques can be categorized as either risk transfer or risk retention.

2-2. Risk transfer shifts the financial consequences of an event to another party through insurance and noninsurance techniques.

2-3. Hedging is practical when it is used to offset the consequences of risk to which one is naturally, voluntarily, or inevitably exposed.

2-4. John could explain to management that they would be substituting a small certain financial cost, the insurance premium, for the possibility of a large uncertain financial loss, paid by the insurer. Insurance is essentially a funded risk transfer. By accepting a premium, the insurer agrees to pay for all of the organization's losses that are covered by the insurance contract. The insurer also agrees to provide services, such as claims handling and defense of liability claims.

C

Assignment 9
Financial Statement Risk Analysis

Assignment 10
Capital Investment and Financial Risk

Assignment 11
Monitoring and Reporting on Risk

Direct Your Learning

Financial Statement Risk Analysis

Educational Objectives

After learning the content of this assignment, you should be able to:

1. Describe the purpose of financial statements.

2. Describe the purpose and content of the balance sheet.

3. Describe the purpose and content of the income statement.

4. Describe the content and purpose of the statement of changes in shareholders' equity and statement of cash flows.

5. Describe the following sources of financial information:
   - Notes to financial statements
   - Securities and Exchange Commission (SEC) filings
   - Company annual reports

6. Apply trend analysis to income statements over multiple periods.

7. Explain how ratio analysis can be used to evaluate liquidity.

8. Describe the components of the typical capital structure for a company.

9. Explain how companies apply financial leverage to increase returns to shareholders.

10. Explain how operating leverage determines the degree to which a business disruption will reduce operating income.

Outline

▶ **Purpose of Financial Statements**

▶ **Balance Sheet**

  A. The Accounting Equation

  B. Assets

  C. Liabilities

  D. Shareholders' Equity

▶ **Income Statement**

  A. Revenue

  B. Expenses

  C. Gross Profit

  D. Operating Income

  E. Net Income

  F. Comprehensive Income

▶ **Statement of Changes in Shareholders' Equity and Statement of Cash Flows**

  A. Statement of Changes in Shareholders' Equity

    1. Paid-in Capital

    2. Retained Earnings

    3. Accumulated Other Comprehensive Income

    4. Treasury Stock

  B. Statement of Cash Flows

    1. Operating Activities

    2. Investing Activities

    3. Financing Activities

▶ **Supplemental Sources of Financial Information**

  A. Notes to Financial Statements

  B. Securities and Exchange Commission Filings

    1. Form 10-K

    2. Form 10-Q

    3. Form 8-K

  C. Company Annual Reports

    1. Report of Management

    2. Management's Discussion and Analysis of Results

▶ **Income Statement Trend Analysis**

  A. Overview of the Procedure

  B. Annual Percentage Change

  C. Interpreting the Results

▶ **Analyzing Liquidity Risk**

  A. Measuring Liquidity

    1. Working Capital

    2. Current Ratio

    3. Acid-Test Ratio

  B. Interpreting the Results of Liquidity Ratio Analysis

▶ **Capital Structure**

  A. Equity

  B. Debt

▶ **Financial Leverage**

  A. Financial Leverage Analysis

    1. Financial Leverage Analysis for Zeselle Company

    2. Tax Shield

  B. Limitations of Financial Leverage

    1. Additional Cost of High Debt

    2. Reduced Cash Flow Flexibility

    3. Cost of Financial Distress

▶ **Operating Leverage**

  A. Analyzing Cost Structure

  B. Operating Leverage Example

 If you find your attention drifting, take a short break to regain your focus.

For each assignment, you should define or describe each of the Key Words and Phrases and answer each of the Review and Application Questions.

Educational Objective 1
Describe the purpose of financial statements.

Key Word or Phrase

Accounting

Review Questions

1-1. Identify activities that are presented quantitatively on an organization's financial statement.

1-2. Describe how financial information typically flows within an organization from the occurrence of financial activity to the reporting on financial statements.

1-3. Identify the purpose of financial statements.

1-4. List individuals who might use information contained in financial statements to make informed financial decisions regarding an organization.

Educational Objective 2
Describe the purpose and content of the balance sheet.

Key Words and Phrases

Current assets

Marketable securities

Receivables

Inventory

Prepaid expenses

Current liabilities

Retained earnings

▶▶

Review Questions

2-1. Explain why shareholders' equity is shown as a liability on the balance sheet.

2-2. Describe noncurrent assets.

2-3. Describe the components of shareholders' equity.

Educational Objective 3
Describe the purpose and content of the income statement.

Key Words and Phrases

Revenue

Gross profit

Gross margin (gross profit margin)

Operating income

Comprehensive income

Review Questions

3-1. Describe the expenses directly related to sales shown on an organization's income statement.

3-2. Describe the general operating expenses shown on an organization's income statement.

3-3. Explain why the income statements of most service operations do not include a cost of goods sold category.

3-4. Explain why the Financial Accounting Standards Board (FASB) created a reporting standard for comprehensive income.

Application Question

3-5. An accountant wishes to recognize as an expense the cost of purchasing inventory. Explain how the accountant would do so.

Educational Objective 4

Describe the content and purpose of the statement of changes in shareholders' equity and statement of cash flows.

Key Words and Phrases

Statement of changes in shareholders' equity

Paid-in capital

Treasury stock

Depreciation expense

Review Questions

4-1. Describe the makeup of the four major components of the statement of changes in shareholders' equity.

a.   Paid-in capital

b.   Retained earnings

c.   Accumulated other comprehensive income

d.   Treasury stock

4-2. Explain the purpose and uses of the statement of cash flows.

Educational Objective 5

Describe the following sources of financial information:

- **Notes to financial statements**
- **Securities and Exchange Commission (SEC) filings**
- **Company annual reports**

Key Words and Phrases

Sarbanes-Oxley Act of 2002

Transparency

Review Questions

5-1. Describe where and when companies record accruals for loss contingencies.

5-2. Describe the events that trigger an 8-K filing with the SEC.

5-3. Explain how an insurance professional may find a company's annual report to be a valuable source of information.

5-4. Describe the three areas of disclosure on the Management Discussion & Analysis (MD&A) for which the Securities and Exchange Commission (SEC) issued interpretive guidelines in response to the Sarbanes-Oxley Act of 2002.

Application Question

5-5. The portfolio manager must make an investment decision on March 15, 20X1. The information in the annual report is as of December 31, 20X0. How can she determine whether any major events affecting the company have occurred since the date of the annual report?

Educational Objective 6
Apply trend analysis to income statements over multiple periods.

Key Word or Phrase
Trend analysis

Review Questions

6-1. Explain the difference between year-to-year analysis and base year-to-date analysis.

6-2. Explain how to calculate the percentage change of an amount from one year to the next.

6-3. Describe the two steps of an income statement trend analysis.

Application Questions

6-4. If Myet Company's revenue climbed from $25,000,000 last year to $35,000,000 this year, what is the annual percentage change between those years?

6-5. If Myet Company's revenue and research and development both increased 40 percent from last year to this year and no other major components of the income statement made a double digit change, what might an analyst conclude?

Educational Objective 7
Explain how ratio analysis can be used to evaluate liquidity.

Key Words and Phrases
Ratio analysis

Liquidity

Working capital

Current ratio

Acid-test ratio (quick ratio)

LIFO method

FIFO method

Review Questions

7-1. Describe liquidity.

7-2. Explain the difference between current assets and current liabilities.

7-3. Explain why the acid-test ratio, or quick ratio, is a more conservative measure of liquidity than the current ratio.

Application Question

7-4. George owns and operates a gym. His business is rapidly growing in membership, but he is concerned about liquidity. The gym's balance sheet indicates its current assets are $500,000 and current liabilities are $400,000. The balance sheet also shows cash, marketable securities, and accounts receivable adding up to $450,000.

   a. What is the gym's working capital and what does that result suggest about the gym's liquidity?

   b. What is the gym's current ratio and what does that result suggest about the gym's liquidity?

   c. What is the gym's acid-text, or quick ratio, and what does that result suggest about the gym's liquidity?

Educational Objective 8

Describe the components of the typical capital structure for a company.

Review Questions

8-1. Explain how a company's capital funds flow in a cycle.

8-2. Describe the debt and equity features of preferred stock.

8-3. Explain why a company may issue preferred stock with a convertible feature, rather than issuing common stock.

8-4. Explain how debt capital is raised.

Educational Objective 9

Explain how companies apply financial leverage to increase returns to shareholders.

Key Word or Phrase

Return on equity (ROE)

Review Questions

9-1.   Describe financial leverage analysis.

9-2.   Explain a potential tax advantage to a company of raising capital using debt rather than equity.

9-3.   Describe three disadvantages a company could experience as a result of raising capital by issuing debt.

Application Question

9-4. Assume that ABC Company has an all-equity capital structure of $8 million and plans a major expansion that will require $2 million. The company currently has earnings before interest and taxes (EBIT) of $1 million and 200,000 common shares outstanding. No taxes are payable. ABC's current earnings per share (EPS) are $5 ($1 million ÷ 200,000 shares), and return on equity (ROE) is 12.5 percent ($1 million profit ÷ $8 million in capital).

The company is considering raising the required funds by either selling common stock or issuing debt. An additional 50,000 common shares could be sold at $40 per share, while debt would require interest at 5 percent, or $100,000 per year. Assume EBIT of $1.2 million. Use financial leverage analysis to compare equity and debt alternatives to raise the additional capital.

Educational Objective 10

Explain how operating leverage determines the degree to which a business disruption will reduce operating income.

Review Questions

10-1. Explain the difference between fixed costs and variable costs.

10-2. Explain the difference between high operating leverage and low operating leverage.

10-3. Explain how a higher level of financial risk for an organization affects its efforts to manage its hazard exposures.

Application Question

10-4. Diana is the owner of a firm that has bid on a government contract to provide an essential service for the country. The government purchasing agent who will decide which firm is awarded the contract has asked Diana to disclose how she structured the firm's costs, specifically what percentage of the costs are variable and what percentage are fixed. Diana has questioned why this is relevant. How would you answer her?

Answers to Assignment 9 Questions

NOTE: These answers are provided to give students a basic understanding of acceptable types of responses. They often are not the only valid answers and are not intended to provide an exhaustive response to the questions.

Educational Objective 1

1-1. Activities that are quantitatively presented on an organization's financial statement include sales, purchases, borrowings, repayments, and investments.

1-2. Financial information typically flows this way within an organization:

    a. Financial activity occurs.

    b. Information regarding the activity is forwarded to the accounting department:

- The activity is recorded using the bookkeeping process.

- The information is classified and analyzed, and the appropriate method of reporting the effects of the bookkeeping records in the financial statements through the accounting process is determined.

- Financial statements are prepared using standardized accounting concepts and principles.

1-3. The purpose of financial statements is to communicate information about an organization's financial activities, and the results of those activities, to individuals who need to make informed financial decisions about the organization.

1-4. Individuals who might use information contained in financial statements to make informed financial decisions regarding an organization include management, investors, insurers, and employees.

Educational Objective 2

2-1. Shareholders' equity is shown on the liabilities side of the balance sheet because a business does not own its net worth. It "owes" its net worth to its owners. The balance sheet must always balance because assets equal liabilities plus shareholders' equity, even if shareholders' equity must be a negative number for balance to occur.

2-2. Noncurrent assets are assets that will be used over a period greater than one year. They are grouped into tangible assets (such as land, buildings, and equipment) and intangible assets. Intangible assets include all assets that cannot be seen or touched, such as leaseholds, patents, copyrights, and trademarks, and are often categorized as intellectual property.

2-3. Shareholders' equity includes the capital contributed by owners and the accumulation of earnings retained by the organization since it was started. Also, for specified assets and liabilities, it includes cumulative changes in value that were not used to calculate cumulative earnings.

Educational Objective 3

3-1. An expense directly related to sales is one that increases or decreases in direct relationship to sales, such as the cost of goods sold, commissions, or the cost of the materials used to ship goods that have been sold.

3-2. A general operating expense is one that is necessary to run the business but bears no direct relationship to the volume of sales, such as a retail store's cost for heating or air conditioning its place of business.

3-3. In a service operation, the cost of goods sold is minimal or nonexistent because no physical product is being sold.

3-4. FASB created a reporting standard for comprehensive income because of concerns that other income of some organizations was materially important to the stakeholders and, therefore, needed to be reported.

3-5. In order to recognize as an expense the cost of purchasing inventory, an accountant would use the cost of goods sold formula to recognize the expense of acquiring goods to sell and coordinate it directly with sales on the income statement. If there are no sales, the ending inventory is equal to the sum of the beginning inventory plus any additions to it. Once an item of inventory has been sold, its cost appears as an expense on the income statement by operation of the cost of goods sold formula.

Educational Objective 4

4-1. These answers describe the makeup of the four major components:

   a. Paid-in capital is the amount of money raised by issuing stock, calculated as the par value of the stock issued plus any additional paid-in capital over the par value.

   b. Retained earnings are the cumulative net income that an organization has retained, after payment of dividends, for reinvestment in the organization's operations. Retained earnings are those used for funding capital expenditures, research and development, or debt repayment. Dividends are deducted from net income to determine the change in retained earnings from one period to the next.

   c. Comprehensive income includes a corporation's net income from the income statement plus other income that is not required to be reported on the income statement. Three components of other comprehensive income include change in unrealized appreciation or depreciation of investments, foreign currency translation gains or losses, and changes in minimum pension liability.

   d. When a corporation buys back its own stock, those shares become treasury stock. The cost of treasury stock is deducted from shareholders' equity because the company used an asset to buy back stock that it had previously issued and it had initially reported the stock payment in the paid-in capital section of shareholders' equity.

4-2. The statement of cash flows is used to identify the sources and uses of cash during the year, essentially reconciling any difference in the beginning and ending balances in the cash account. This statement is used to determine an organization's ability to generate positive future cash flows, its ability to meet its financial obligations, and its need for additional financing. It is also used to determine the reasons for any differences between net income and associated cash receipts and disbursements, such as those resulting from loan proceeds or repayments, increases or decreases in accounts receivable, or depreciation expense.

Educational Objective 5

5-1. Companies record accruals for loss contingencies directly to the balance sheet and income statement when it is probable that a liability (loss) has been incurred and the amount can be reasonably estimated.

5-2. Events that trigger an 8-K filing include these:

- Material definitive agreements entered into or terminated that are not in the ordinary course of the company's business, such as a definitive agreement to sell a significant operating division to an unrelated company

- Release of nonpublic information about a company's financial condition

- Creation of a direct financial obligation (such as a long-term operating lease) under an off-balance sheet arrangement—that is, an arrangement that does not have to be recorded in the financial statements

- Change of independent auditor certifying the financial statements

- Departure or election of directors and departure or appointment of principal officers

5-3. Insurance professionals find the annual report to be a valuable source of information about the company's business purpose and philosophy, its financial results, and its direction for the future. This information helps provide a general background for making specific underwriting decisions.

5-4. The Sarbanes-Oxley Act of 2002 prompted the SEC to issue interpretive guidance for improved MD&A disclosure in three areas:

- Liquidity and capital resources, including off-balance sheet arrangements, contractual agreements, and contingent liabilities

- Certain trading activities involving non-exchange-traded contracts accounted for at fair market value, including buying or selling private securities

- Relationships and transactions with persons or entities that derive benefits from nonindependent relationships with the company or the company's related parties

5-5. To determine whether any major events have occurred that affected the company since the publication of its annual report, the portfolio manager should obtain a copy of any Form 8-K that the company has filed with the SEC since the end of 20X0. Form 8-K is the current report that publically traded companies must file with the SEC to announce any major events that shareholders should know about. The form must be filed within four business days of the triggering event.

Educational Objective 6

6-1. Year-to-year analysis determines the percentage change in values for statement items between consecutive years in the period under consideration. Base-year-to-date analysis uses the earliest year of the period under consideration as a base year and determines the percentage change in statement item values for each successive year relative to that base year.

6-2. To calculate the percentage change of an amount from one year to the next, divide the change from the first year to the subsequent year by the first year amount, and multiply the result by 100 to express it as a percentage.

6-3. The first step is to calculate the percentage change of an amount from one year to the next on selected components of an organization's income statements over several years to produce an annual percentage change income statement. The second step is to interpret the results.

6-4. ($35,000,000 – $25,000,000) divided by $25,000,000 = (0.4) = 40 percent increase

6-5. An analyst might conclude the increased expenditure in research and development paid off in a corresponding increase in revenue. The management of Myet may want to further support expenditures in research and development if additional revenue can be generated in similar proportions.

Educational Objective 7

7-1. Liquidity refers to a company's ability to convert assets to cash to satisfy its obligations.

7-2. Current assets are cash and assets that are likely to be converted to cash within one year of the balance sheet date—primarily marketable securities, accounts receivable, and inventory. Current liabilities are obligations that will need to be paid within the same one-year period, including accounts payable; the current portion of loans payable; and accrued expenses such as wages payable, interest payable, and taxes payable.

7-3. The acid-test ratio, or quick ratio, is a more conservative measure of liquidity than the current ratio because it includes only cash, marketable securities, and accounts receivable in its numerator.

7-4. These answers address George's case:

a. The working capital is determined by subtracting current liabilities from current assets ($400,000 from $500,000). The gym's working capital is a positive $100,000, which is an indication that it has adequate liquidity. Most businesses have a positive working capital. This result may be compared with other businesses' in the industry to learn if it is in line with the industry.

b. The current ratio is determined by dividing current assets by current liabilities ($500,000 by $400,000). The result for George's gym is 1.25. A number greater than one is encouraging because it is another indication that it has adequate liquidity but, again, should be compared with other businesses' in the same industry for additional interpretation of the result.

c. The acid-test, or quick ratio, is determined by dividing the sum of cash, marketable securities, and accounts receivable ($450,000 for the gym) by current liabilities ($400,000). The resulting 1.125 for the gym indicates that the gym's current assets, not including inventory, are still greater than its current liabilities. This is yet another indication that it has adequate liquidity. Inventory is a relatively low amount because the gym is primarily an exercise facility for its members and does not sell many products. As a result, the acid-test results are close to the current ratio results; both should be compared with industry benchmarks for additional interpretation.

Educational Objective 8

8-1. A company's capital funds flow in this cycle:

- The company sells common stock (equity), bonds (debt), or some other type of security in the capital market and receives cash.

- Proceeds from the security's sale are used to purchase assets.

- Cash returns from the assets can be retained in the company to finance operations or to finance the purchase of more assets.

- Ultimately, cash returns can be distributed to the suppliers of capital.

- Debt holders receive income in the form of interest payments, and equity holders can receive income as cash dividends.

8-2. Preferred stock has features of both debt and equity. It can resemble debt if its dividend is a fixed obligation (either a stated percentage of the par value of the preferred share or a stated dollar amount per share). Preferred stock, like common stock, creates an equity interest in whatever profits remain after all other expenses and creditors have been paid. It can resemble debt except that omission of a dividend does not result in the entire issue becoming payable immediately, as would a bond.

8-3. Some preferred stock, like some debt securities, is convertible into common stock under terms and conditions specified at the time of issue. This feature is used when the company wants to sell common stock to increase capital, but when selling is not economical because the company's stock price is depressed.

8-4. Debt capital is usually raised through the sale of bonds in the capital market. If the bonds are backed simply by the general assets of the corporation (that is, they carry no specific pledge of assets), they are referred to as debentures.

Educational Objective 9

9-1. Financial leverage analysis is a technique used to compare earnings per share (EPS) under alternate capitalization plans with varying levels of debt and equity.

9-2. Under federal tax law, interest on debt is deductible in calculating taxable income, but dividends paid to stockholders are not. As a result, more after-tax money is available to the company if it raises capital using debt rather than equity.

9-3. The first disadvantage a company may encounter by issuing debt is that lenders typically require higher interest rates as debt increases. Also, future investments could offer lower returns than prior investments. Higher costs and lower returns could reduce the benefits of leverage, or even result in a loss for the company. The second disadvantage a company may encounter is a reduction in the flexibility that management has in managing cash and an increase in the company's liquidity risk. The third disadvantage a company may encounter is that as its ratio of debt to equity rises, it will experience an increased risk of defaulting on its debt and an increased potential for bankruptcy.

9-4. ABC Company's EPS is higher under the debt alternative than under the equity alternative. Return on equity is also higher using the debt alternative. Even though net income was reduced because of the interest expense from using debt, less equity was needed to finance ABC Company's operations.

	Equity	Debt (Financial Leverage)
Income Statement:		
EBIT	$ 1,200,000	$ 1,200,000
Interest Expense	0	100,000
Net Income (NI)	$ 1,200,000	$ 1,100,000
Balance Sheet:		
Assets	$10,000,000	$10,000,000
Liabilities	0	$ 2,000,000
Equity	10,000,000	8,000,000
Total (Liabilities and Shareholders' Equity)	$10,000,000	$10,000,000
Common Shares Outstanding (CSO)	250,000	200,000
Return on Equity (NI ÷ Equity)	12.0%	13.8%
Earnings per Share (NI ÷ CSO)	$ 4.80	$ 5.50

Educational Objective 10

10-1. Fixed costs are incurred in the production of products or services and do not change when the amount of products or services produced changes; examples include rent, property tax, and interest. In contrast, variable costs are those expenses that do change when the amount of products or services that are produced changes, such as direct labor and raw materials.

10-2. If an organization chooses to structure its costs with a high percentage of fixed costs and a low percentage of variable costs, it is considered to have high operating leverage. This means the high percentage of fixed costs of the organization's cost structure will be leveraged to make its operating profit more volatile. A small increase in the amount of sales can cause a relatively large increase in operating income. In contrast, an organization with a low percentage of fixed costs and a high percentage of variable costs has a low operating leverage. This means the low percentage of fixed costs of the organization's cost structure will be leveraged to make its operating profit less volatile. A small increase in the amount of sales can cause a relatively small increase in operating income.

10-3. When an organization is faced with a higher level of financial risk, the organization must make a greater effort in managing its hazard risk exposures to alleviate or compensate for the additional financial risk.

10-4. What percentage of Diana's costs are variable and what percentage are fixed is relevant because the higher the percentage of her costs that are fixed (versus variable), the higher the operating leverage. The higher the operating leverage, the higher the volatility of operating profits. The higher the volatility of operating profits, the higher the financial risk for the firm. The contract is for an essential service of the government, so it has a vested interest in the viability of Diana's firm.

Direct Your Learning

Capital Investment and Financial Risk

Educational Objectives

After learning the content of this assignment, you should be able to:

1. Calculate the present value of a future payment.

2. Calculate the present value of an annuity, given the applicable rate of return and number of periods.

3. Calculate the present value of unequal payments, given the applicable rate of return and number of periods over which the payments will be spread.

4. Calculate the net present value of a series of cash outflows and inflows, given the applicable rate of return and number of periods.

5. Evaluate capital investment proposals using the net present value method.

6. Calculate the net present value of a capital investment proposal, taking into account accidental losses and loss prevention.

7. Calculate the effect on net income of a call option that offsets input price increases.

Outline

▶ **Present Value and Discounting**
  A. Present Value Over a Single Period
  B. Present Value Over Multiple Periods
▶ **Present Value of an Annuity**
▶ **Present Value of Unequal Payments**
▶ **Net Present Value**
▶ **Evaluating Capital Investment Proposals**
  A. Capital Budgeting and Expenditures
  B. NPV Method
  C. Cash Flow Analysis
▶ **Evaluating Cash Flows From Treating Hazard Risk**
  A. Case Facts
  B. Overview of Steps
  C. Cash Flow Analysis Recognizing Expected Losses
  D. Cash Flow Analysis With Loss Prevention or
      Reduction
▶ **Using Call Options to Limit Financial Risk**
  A. Case Facts
  B. Underlying Concepts
  C. Transferring Wheat Price Increases

Studying before sleeping helps you retain material better than studying before undertaking other tasks.

For each assignment, you should define or describe each of the Key Words and Phrases and answer each of the Review and Application Questions.

Educational Objective 1
Calculate the present value of a future payment.

Key Words and Phrases

Present value

Discounting

Discount rate

Review Questions

1-1. Explain why money received in the future must be a higher amount than money received presently to be of the same value.

1-2. Describe what "n" and "r" represent in the present value formula.

1-3. List the three ways to calculate the present value of an amount of money.

Application Questions

1-4. At the end of one year, $20,000 needs to be in a savings account that pays 3 percent interest compounded annually. Using the present value formula, determine how much to deposit in the account today to have the required $20,000 in one year.

1-5. An organization has a receivable totaling $31,500 that is due three years from today. The financial manager must choose between receiving full payment of $31,500 in three years or accepting a reduced payment today in full settlement of the receivable. Assuming the money, if received today, could be deposited in an account that earns 3 percent interest for three years, what is the smallest amount the financial manager can accept today to make the second option an acceptable alternative?

1-6. Use the present value table to calculate the present value in each of the following scenarios.

$$PV = FV_n \div (1 + r)^n$$

	Interest Rate (r)				
Period (n)	1%	2%	3%	4%	5%
1	0.9901	0.9804	0.9709	0.9615	0.9524
2	0.9803	0.9612	0.9426	0.9246	0.9070
3	0.9706	0.9423	0.9151	0.8890	0.8638
4	0.9610	0.9238	0.8885	0.8548	0.8227
5	0.9515	0.9057	0.8626	0.8219	0.7835

a. At the end of one year, $11,500 needs to be in a savings account that pays 3 percent interest compounded annually. Using the present value table, determine how much to deposit in the account today to have $11,500 in one year.

b. Using the present value table, calculate the present value of $15,000 received three years from now at a discount rate of 3 percent.

Educational Objective 2
Calculate the present value of an annuity, given the applicable rate of return and number of periods.

Key Word or Phrase
Annuity

Application Questions

2-1. At the end of one year, $20,000 needs to be in a savings account that pays 3 percent interest compounded annually. Determine how much should be deposited in the account today to have the required $20,000 in one year.

2-2. An organization has a receivable totaling $31,500 that is due today. The financial manager must make a choice between receiving full payment of $31,500 today or accepting two end of the year installments of $16,500. Assuming the money, if received today, could be deposited in an account that earns 3 percent interest for two years, should the financial manager chose the payment today of $31,500 or $16,500 paid each year for two years?

2-3. A company receives an annuity payment of $15,000 each year for three years at a discount rate of 3 percent. Find the present value of the annuity in the specified scenario by multiplying the annuity payment per period by the present value of an annuity factor in the annuity table.

Period (n)	Interest Rate (r)									
	1%	2%	3%	4%	5%	6%	7%	8%	9%	10%
1	0.9901	0.9804	0.9709	0.9615	0.9524	0.9434	0.9346	0.9259	0.9174	0.9091
2	1.9704	1.9416	1.9135	1.8861	1.8594	1.8334	1.8080	1.7833	1.7591	1.7355
3	2.9410	2.8839	2.8286	2.7751	2.7232	2.6730	2.6243	2.5771	2.5313	2.4869
4	3.9020	3.8077	3.7171	3.6299	3.5460	3.4651	3.3872	3.3121	3.2397	3.1699
5	4.8534	4.7135	4.5797	4.4518	4.3295	4.2124	4.1002	3.9927	3.8897	3.7908
6	5.7955	5.6014	5.4172	5.2421	5.0757	4.9173	4.7665	4.6229	4.4859	4.3553
7	6.7282	6.4720	6.2303	6.0021	5.7864	5.5824	5.3893	5.2064	5.0330	4.8684
8	7.6517	7.3255	7.0197	6.7327	6.4632	6.2098	5.9713	5.7466	5.5348	5.3349
9	8.5660	8.1622	7.7861	7.4353	7.1078	6.8017	6.5152	6.2469	5.9952	5.7590
10	9.4713	8.9826	8.5302	8.1109	7.7217	7.3601	7.0236	6.7101	6.4177	6.1446

Educational Objective 3

Calculate the present value of unequal payments, given the applicable rate of return and number of periods over which the payments will be spread.

Review Question

3-1. What constitutes the present value of a stream of unequal payments?

Application Question

3-2. An individual is offered $500 one year from now, $600 two years from now, $1,000 three years from now, and $1,400 four years from now. Assuming a 3 percent interest rate, use the present value table to calculate the present value of this future stream of payments.

Interest Rate (r)

Period (n)	1%	2%	3%	4%	5%	6%	7%	8%	9%	10%
1	0.9901	0.9804	0.9709	0.9615	0.9524	0.9434	0.9346	0.9259	0.9174	0.9091
2	0.9803	0.9612	0.9426	0.9246	0.9070	0.8900	0.8734	0.8573	0.8417	0.8264
3	0.9706	0.9423	0.9151	0.8890	0.8638	0.8396	0.8163	0.7938	0.7722	0.7513
4	0.9610	0.9238	0.8885	0.8548	0.8227	0.7921	0.7629	0.7350	0.7084	0.6830
5	0.9515	0.9057	0.8626	0.8219	0.7835	0.7473	0.7130	0.6806	0.6499	0.6209

Educational Objective 4

Calculate the net present value of a series of cash outflows and inflows, given the applicable rate of return and number of periods.

Key Word or Phrase

Net present value (NPV)

Review Questions

4-1. What is an investment's net present value (NPV)?

4-2. Describe the NPV rule.

4-3. How does an organization investing in a project determine its required rate of return?

4-4. Identify three limitations of NPV analysis.

Application Question

4-5. A company's risk management professional is determining whether to invest $8,000 today in a three-year safety campaign to reduce occupational injuries. The company requires a rate of return of 5 percent. It expects to save injury-related expenses of $1,500 at the end of the first year, $2,500 at the end of the second year, and $4,800 at the end of the third year. Use the present value table and the NPV rule to determine whether the investment should be made.

Interest Rate (r)

Period (n)	1%	2%	3%	4%	5%	6%	7%	8%	9%	10%
1	0.9901	0.9804	0.9709	0.9615	0.9524	0.9434	0.9346	0.9259	0.9174	0.9091
2	0.9803	0.9612	0.9426	0.9246	0.9070	0.8900	0.8734	0.8573	0.8417	0.8264
3	0.9706	0.9423	0.9151	0.8890	0.8638	0.8396	0.8163	0.7938	0.7722	0.7513
4	0.9610	0.9238	0.8885	0.8548	0.8227	0.7921	0.7629	0.7350	0.7084	0.6830
5	0.9515	0.9057	0.8626	0.8219	0.7835	0.7473	0.7130	0.6806	0.6499	0.6209

Educational Objective 5

Evaluate capital investment proposals using the net present value method.

Key Words and Phrases

Capital budgeting

Operating expenditures

Capital expenditures

Salvage value

Risk-return trade-off

Differential (incremental) annual after-tax net cash flow

Straight-line depreciation method

Sensitivity analysis

Review Questions

5-1. Identify the information required to evaluate capital investment proposals using the net present value (NPV) method.

5-2. Explain why cost of capital is not the only consideration when using the NPV method to determine minimum acceptable rate of return.

5-3. Explain why organizations not subject to income taxes have simplified cash flow calculations compared with for-profit organizations using cash flow analysis.

5-4. Explain why sensitivity analysis is most accurate when all variables except the one being analyzed are held constant.

Application Question

5-5. Sally runs a not-for-profit charity organization that is not subject to income tax. She is considering a capital investment proposal that has 1) an initial investment requirement of $100,000, 2) an acceptable rate of return of 10 percent, 3) annual net cash flows of $21,000 for seven years, 4) no salvage value, and 5) a present value factor of 4.868 (the result of $1 received annually at the end of each year for seven years at 10 percent interest compounded annually). Is the NPV method of this proposal positive or negative?

Educational Objective 6

Calculate the net present value of a capital investment proposal, taking into account accidental losses and loss prevention.

Application Question

6-1. Milker Corporation is considering buying Prairie View Farm, a family-operated dairy farm. The farm's $300,000 annual revenue is derived from sales of unprocessed milk. Each year some customers claim to have been poisoned by the milk, and, because Prairie View milk is unprocessed, the farm is particularly vulnerable to liability. Therefore, rather than go to court, the farm has been paying an average of $20,000 annually to settle these claims.

For an additional $100,000, Milker can purchase equipment for the farm that will process its milk (which would result in reducing the settlements for poison milk claims to $5,000 annually) for the next 15 years, after which the equipment will have no salvage value. The equipment would need $1,000 in maintenance annually.

The purchase price for Prairie View Farm is $1,500,000. Milker believes that the farm will be productive for 15 years and will then shut down and have no salvage value. Milker's management has established that its minimum acceptable rate of return annually is 8 percent. Milker's tax rate is 35 percent.

Determine whether Milker should buy this farm, taking into consideration the expected losses and loss prevention device. Show your calculations.

Educational Objective 7

Calculate the effect on net income of a call option that offsets input price increases.

Key Word or Phrase

Forward contract

Application Question

7-1. Dana is a home builder who relies on timber and lumber to build homes. The price of lumber changes over time. Dana is uncomfortable with the swing in his company's monthly net income that results from the changing price of timber. To reduce the largely unpredictable fluctuations in timber prices and monthly operating results, Dana is considering hedging his business risk through the use of a call option.

These are the facts needed to calculate the effect on net income of a call option that offsets input price increases for this company: Dana needs an average of 4,000 units of lumber each month; the current market price of a unit of lumber is $8; the strike price (the price set in a call option contract) of a unit of lumber is $8; the call fee is $500; the purchase price of the call option contract is $4,000; the selling price of a call (high) is $12,000; and the selling price of a call (low) is $0.

With Hedging $8 Call	Lumber Prices Stay at $8	Lumber Prices Rise to $10
Revenues		
Sales	$75,000	$75,000
Other income	$ 5,000	$ 5,000
Net income on call option	$ 0	$ 8,000
Total Revenues	$80,000	$88,000
Expenses		
Lumber	$32,000	$40,000
Other expenses	$30,000	$30,000
Call fee	$ 500	$ 500
Loss on call option	$ 4,000	$ 0
Total Expenses	($66,500)	($70,500)
Net Income	$13,500	

a. Explain why Dana would be willing to give up a potential net income increase from falling lumber prices by spending money on the purchase of a call option contract.

b. Calculate the net income on the call option Dana would receive if the price of lumber rose to $10 per unit in a particular month for all the units of lumber needed to produce the homes that Dana plans to sell during the month.

c. Calculate the overall result for Dana using the call option contract to hedge lumber prices at $8 if the price of lumber rises to $10 per unit.

Answers to Assignment 10 Questions

NOTE: These answers are provided to give students a basic understanding of acceptable types of responses. They often are not the only valid answers and are not intended to provide an exhaustive response to the questions.

Educational Objective 1

1-1. Because a sum of money grows over time by earning a return (for example, interest on a bond investment), its present value is less than its future value.

1-2. In the present value formula, "n" is the number of periods and "r" is the rate of return.

1-3. The three ways to calculate present value are these:

- Using a present value formula

- Using a financial (present value) table

- Using a financial calculator and/or a computer spreadsheet program

1-4. The amount to deposit can be calculated in this manner:

$$PV = FV_n \div (1 + r)^n$$

$$= \$20,000 \div (1 + 0.03)^1$$

$$= \$20,000 \div 1.03$$

$$= \$19,417$$

1-5. The smallest amount the financial manager can accept today can be determined by calculating the present value of $31,500:

$$PV = FV_n \div (1 + r)^n$$

$$= \$31,500 \div (1 + 0.03)^3$$

$$= \$31,500 \div 1.0927$$

$$= \$28,828$$

The present value of $31,500 received three years from now at a discount rate of 3 percent is $28,828. Therefore, the financial manager determines that at least $28,828 must be received today to make the second option of a reduced settlement an acceptable alternative.

1-6. These answers give the present values:

a. Using the present value table, the present value (PV) of $11,500 deposited in an account for one year at 3 percent interest would be calculated in this way:

$$PV = FV_n \times PV \text{ factor } (r = 3\%, n = 1 \text{ year})$$

$$= \$11,500 \times 0.9709$$

$$= \$11,165$$

b. Using the present value table, the present value of $15,000 received three years from now at a discount rate of 3 percent would be calculated in this manner:

$$PV = FV_n \times PV\,\text{factor} \ (r = 3\%, \ n = 3 \ \text{years})$$
$$= \$15{,}000 \times 0.9151$$
$$= \$13{,}727$$

Educational Objective 2

2-1.

The amount to deposit may be calculated as shown:

$$PV = FV_n \div (1 + r)^n$$
$$= \$20{,}000 \div (1 + 0.03)^1$$
$$= \$20{,}000 \div 1.03$$
$$= \$19{,}417$$

2-2.

The formula for finding the present value of an annuity is $PV = FV_n \div (1 + r)^n$. Here r equals 3 and n equals 2.

$$\$16{,}500 \div (1 + 0.03) = \$16{,}012$$
$$\$16{,}500 \div (1 + 0.03)^2 = \$15{,}553$$
$$= \$31{,}565$$

The financial manager should choose to collect the receivable as two annual installments of $16,500 as the present value of those two installments is greater than the present value $31,500 today.

2-3.

Using the annuity factor in the annuity table, the present value of $15,000 received each year for three years at a discount rate of 3 percent would be calculated as shown:

$$PVA = A \times PVAF$$

Here, A equals annuity payment per period and $PVAF$ equals present value annuity factor.

The $PVAF$ for $r = 3$ and $n = 3$ is 2.8286

$$= \$15{,}000 \times 2.8286$$
$$= \$42{,}429$$

Educational Objective 3

3-1. The present value of a stream of unequal payments is the sum of the present values of the individual payments.

3-2. The present value of each individual payment is calculated by multiplying it by the corresponding present value factor from the present value table and then summing the individual present values:

(1)	(2)	(3)	(4) = (2) × (3)
Year	Payments	Present Value Factor	Present Value
1	$500	0.9709	$ 485.45
2	600	0.9426	565.56
3	1,000	0.9151	915.10
4	1,400	0.8885	1,243.90
			$3,210.01

Educational Objective 4

4-1.   An investment's NPV is the difference between the present value of its cash inflows and the present value of its cash outflows.

4-2.   The NPV rule dictates that an investment should be made only if its NPV is greater than zero.

4-3.   The organization investing in a project usually sets its required rate of return equal to its cost of capital so as to accept only investments that cover its cost of funds.

4-4.   Some of the limitations of NPV analysis that should be considered are these:

- The amounts and timing of cash flows may differ from those expected over the life of an investment.

- NPV analysis does not formally factor in the effect of uncertainty (risk) with respect to future cash flows, losses, discount rates, or time horizons.

- NPV analysis focuses on maximizing economic value and disregards an organization's nonfinancial goals and other stakeholders' interests.

4-5.   The present value of each payment may be calculated by multiplying the payment amount by the appropriate present value factor. The present value factor lies at the intersection of the corresponding period and interest rate. The corresponding periods are one, two, and three, respectively, and the corresponding interest rate is 5 percent:

Year	Payment	Present Value Factor	Present Value (Payment × Present Value Factor)
0	−$8,000	1.0000	−$8,000.00
1	$1,500	0.9524	1,428.60
2	$2,500	0.9070	2,267.50
3	$4,800	0.8638	4,146.24
Net Present Value (NPV)			−$157.66

Because this investment's NPV is negative, the NPV rule suggests that the organization should not make this investment because the present value of its cash inflows does not exceed the present value of its cash outflow.

Educational Objective 5

5-1. To evaluate capital investment proposals using the NPV method, this information is required:

- Amount of the initial investment

- Acceptable annual rate of return

- Amount and timing of the differential (incremental) annual after-tax net cash flows associated with the proposal over its estimated useful life

- Salvage value (if any) of the investment

5-2. Cost of capital is not the only consideration when using the NPV method to determine minimum acceptable rate of return. A risk-averse financial officer of an organization will demand a higher rate of return from an investment proposal that has a higher risk. This is known as the risk-return trade-off, and it requires investors to determine the appropriate balance between assuming the lowest possible risk and achieving the highest possible return.

5-3. In for-profit organizations, income taxes are cash outflows and must be deducted from cash revenues to calculate net cash flows. Taxes are treated like any other cash outlay, with income taxes calculated as a percentage of taxable income. Taxable income is based on some cash and some noncash revenues and expenses. For organizations not subject to income taxes, these noncash revenues and expenses can be ignored, simplifying cash flow calculations.

5-4. When all variables except the one being analyzed are held constant, a sensitivity analysis is most accurate. This is because the NPV can be measured to see how sensitive it is to changes in that variable.

5-5. The first step in determining whether the NPV of Sally's proposal is positive or negative is to establish the present value of the differential inflows: $21,000 multiplied by the present value factor of 4.868, or $102,228. The second step is to subtract the present value of the initial investment, $100,000, from the present value of the differential inflows, $102,228. This results in a positive NPV of $2,228.

Educational Objective 6

6-1. The Prairie View Farm investment proposal can be evaluated in this way:

Investment Proposal of Milker Corporation buying Prairie View Farm
Net Cash Flow (NCF) Calculations

Differential cash revenues		$300,000
Less: cash expenses (except income taxes)		
Expected value of milk poisoning claims	$5,000	
Milk processing equipment maintenance	$1,000	($6,000)
Before-tax NCF		$294,000
Less: income taxes		
Before-tax NCF	$294,000	
Less: Depreciation expense ($1,600,000 divided by 15 years)	($106,667)	
Taxable income	$187,333	
Income taxes (35% multiplied by $187,333)		($65,567)
After-tax NCF		$228,433
NCF Evaluation		
Factors:		
Initial investment	$1,600,000	
Life of project	15 years	
Annual after-tax NCF	$228,433	
Minimum acceptable rate of return (annual)	8%	
Evaluation by net present value (NPV) method:		
Present value of NCF ($228,433 multiplied by 8.56)	$1,955,389	
Less: Present value of initial investment	($1,600,000)	
NPV	$355,389	

With a positive NPV, the proposal is acceptable. Milker should consider purchasing Prairie View Farm.

Educational Objective 7

7-1. These answers relate to Dana's home building company:

a.   The purpose of incurring the expense of a call option contract is to protect against losses from rising lumber prices. This approach would give Dana greater assurance that his monthly net income will be consistent despite any change in the cost of lumber.

b. As the lumber price rises during the month, Dana may be able to sell this lumber call option for $12,000, making an $8,000 ($12,000 – $4,000) net income. The brokerage firm handling Dana's purchase and sale of the lumber call must be paid its call fee of $500. Subtracting the call fee of $500 results in revenue of $7,500 to be applied toward the increased lumber expense.

c. The overall result that will fit in at the bottom of the exhibit in the column farthest to the right is a $17,500 net income, which is relatively close to the $13,500 net income that Dana would have earned had the price of lumber remained at $8.

Direct Your Learning

Monitoring and Reporting on Risk

Educational Objectives

After learning the content of this assignment, you should be able to:

1. Describe the responsibilities and functions of an organization's board of directors in providing effective risk management oversight.

2. Explain how organizational environment and internal control techniques support risk monitoring efforts.

3. Explain how the responsibilities and functions of an internal audit differ from those of internal controls and how an internal audit provides support to an organization's risk monitoring efforts.

4. Describe risk assurance methods that advise an organization of its risk management performance level.

5. Identify the elements of effective risk management reports.

Outline

▶ **Board Risk Oversight**

A. Board Responsibility for Risk Management Oversight

B. Risk Management Reporting

  1. Board Risk Committee

  2. Chief Risk Officer (CRO)

  3. Transparency and Clear Communications

C. Internal Audits

  1. Internal Audit Committee Formal Reports

  2. Internal Audit Committee Informal Reports

▶ **Internal Controls Support to Risk Monitoring**

A. Internal Controls Defined

  1. Purpose of Internal Controls

  2. Benefits of Internal Controls

  3. COSO's Five Components

B. Internal Controls Within the Organizational Environment

  1. Board Responsibilities

  2. Management Responsibilities

  3. Employee Responsibilities

  4. Auditor Responsibilities

  5. Transparent Communications

C. Internal Control Techniques

D. Internal Control Linked to Risk Monitoring

  1. Benefits of Risk Monitoring

  2. Limitations of Risk Monitoring

▶ **Internal Audit Support to Risk Monitoring**

A. Defining Internal Audit

  1. Functions and Responsibilities

  2. Use of Internal Controls

  3. Independent Status

B. Benefits to the Organization

  1. Report Assurance

  2. Report Certification

C. Risk Management and Internal Audit

  1. Role of Risk Management

  2. Role of Internal Auditor

D. Risk-Based Auditing

  1. Audit to Business Objectives

  2. Focus on the Materiality of the Risk

  3. Identify the Threats to the Achievement of the Business Goals and Objectives

▶ **Risk Assurance to Evaluate Risk Management Performance**

A. Risk Assurance

  1. Risk Assurance Sources

  2. Risk Management Effectiveness

B. Control Risk Self-Assessment

C. Risk Assurance Benefits

▶ **Risk Management Monitoring and Reporting**

A. Risk Reporting

  1. Characteristics

  2. Functionality

B. Managing Data

  1. Integrated Reporting Versus Silo Reporting

  2. Quantitative Data Versus Qualitative Data

C. Report Formats

  1. Best Concepts

  2. Dashboards and Scorecards

 Try to establish a study area away from any distractions, to be used only for studying.

For each assignment, you should define or describe each of the Key Words and Phrases and answer each of the Review and Application Questions.

Educational Objective 1

Describe the responsibilities and functions of an organization's board of directors in providing effective risk management oversight.

Review Questions

1-1. Identify examples of the broad categories of risk that a board must oversee.

1-2. Identify examples of the laws and regulations created to address board oversight of risk management in the wake of the global financial crisis of the late 2000s.

1-3. Identify the purpose of a board's audit committee.

1-4. Identify the common principles followed by risk committees.

1-5. Identify the primary difference between an audit committee's and a separate risk committee's oversight of risk management.

Educational Objective 2

Explain how organizational environment and internal control techniques support risk monitoring efforts.

Review Questions

2-1. Identify the three categories into which the Committee of Sponsoring Organizations of the Treadway Commission (COSO) groups internal control objectives.

2-2. Identify examples of the ways that internal controls can reduce uncertainty within an organization.

2-3. Identify the five interrelated components of internal controls listed in the COSO framework.

2-4. Identify examples of hard controls.

2-5. Identify examples of soft controls.

Application Question

2-6. An organization wishes to determine whether a recent change in its leave-time policies has affected employee morale. Explain whether this determination entails hard control or soft control and suggest a manner in which it could be made.

Educational Objective 3

Explain how the responsibilities and functions of an internal audit differ from those of internal controls and how an internal audit provides support to an organization's risk monitoring efforts.

Review Questions

3-1. Identify the purpose of an internal audit department.

3-2. Identify how an internal audit benefits an organization.

3-3. Describe the manner in which the internal audit is evolving.

3-4. Identify the elements for which the risk management team is held responsible in the risk management function.

3-5. Identify the three principles on which successful risk-based auditing focuses.

Educational Objective 4
Describe risk assurance methods that advise an organization of its risk management performance level.

Review Questions

4-1. Identify the organizational characteristics associated with a high level of risk assurance.

4-2. Identify examples of organizational sources of risk assurance.

4-3. Identify examples of external sources of risk assurance.

4-4. Identify the purpose of the Control Risk Self-Assessment (CRSA) model.

4-5. Identify the benefits of risk assurance to internal and external stakeholders.

Application Question

4-6. An organization is seeking assurance regarding whether risk controls are in place and functioning as designed. Identify the risk assurance source that could help the organization make such a determination.

Educational Objective 5
Identify the elements of effective risk management reports.

Review Questions

5-1. Identify the key design features that risk management monitoring and reporting must incorporate.

5-2. Identify examples of reports generated by a risk monitoring and reporting system.

5-3.   Describe the characteristics of effective risk reports.

5-4.   Identify two kinds of choices to be aware of in managing the data reporting process.

5-5.   Identify features and concepts that some organizations find useful in a report format.

Answers to Assignment 11 Questions

NOTE: These answers are provided to give students a basic understanding of acceptable types of responses. They often are not the only valid answers and are not intended to provide an exhaustive response to the questions.

Educational Objective 1

1-1. Broad categories of risk that a board must oversee include these:

   • Strategic risks that arise from trends in the economy and society

   • Operational risks that arise from people, processes, systems, or controls

   • Financial risks that arise from the effect of market forces on financial assets or liabilities

1-2. Laws and regulations created to address board oversight of risk management in the wake of the global financial crisis of the late 2000s include these:

   • The Dodd-Frank Act

   • The United States Securities and Exchange Commission (SEC) Rule 33-9089

   • The 2010 update to the United Kingdom Corporate Governance Code

   • The European Union's European Systemic Risk Board

1-3. The purpose of a board's audit committee is to assess the organization's compliance with its stated internal procedures and financial reporting systems as well as with regulatory and legal requirements.

1-4. These are the common principles followed by risk committees:

   • Ensuring that a risk management process is in place at all levels of the organization and that the risk management process is being followed

   • Identifying and quantifying risks within the organization

   • Defining the organization's risk appetite and tolerance

   • Prioritizing the selection of risks to determine those that should be retained within the organization and those that should be reduced, eliminated, or transferred

1-5. The primary difference between an audit committee's and a separate risk committee's oversight of risk management is that the audit committee's focus is on complying with existing standards, while the risk committee's focus is likely on setting new and appropriate standards and evaluating existing standards.

Educational Objective 2

2-1. These are the three categories into which the Committee of Sponsoring Organizations of the Treadway Commission (COSO) groups internal control objectives:

- Effectiveness and efficiency of operations objectives

- Reporting objectives

- Compliance objectives

2-2. These are examples of the ways that internal controls can reduce uncertainty within an organization:

- Internal controls establish clear lines of authority and responsibility for risk management at all levels of the organization.

- Internal controls generate communication among all levels of management and within departments.

- Effective internal controls promote a risk management culture and help the organization to efficiently allocate internal risk management resources.

2-3. The COSO framework lists five interrelated components of internal controls:

- Control environment

- Risk assessment

- Control activities

- Information and communication

- Monitoring

2-4. Examples of hard controls include process checklists, corporate policies and procedures manuals, lines of authority, physical controls like fire alarms and safes, performance reports, and equipment condition reports.

2-5. Examples of soft controls include an organization's core values and ethics, risk management philosophy, collegiality among its stakeholders, and commitment to excellence.

2-6. This determination entails a soft control because employee morale is an intangible quality that deals with people's attitudes and beliefs. Employee meetings or open forums with senior management or board members may turn up employee dissatisfaction issues. Alternatively, the organizations could use surveys to measure employee attitudes.

Educational Objective 3

3-1. The purpose of an internal audit department is to evaluate how well an organization is achieving its business objectives.

3-2. An internal audit benefits an organization by ensuring that financial reports are accurate and that the appropriate risk disclosures are reported.

3-3. The internal audit is evolving away from being primarily a financial controls evaluation process; it's becoming a more holistic system of reviewing an organization's overall objectives and evaluating the risks that challenge the organization's ability to meet those objectives.

3-4. The risk management team is held accountable for the proper design and implementation of the risk management plan, internal controls, and overall success of the risk management effort.

3-5. Successful risk-based auditing focuses on these three principles:

- Audit to business objectives

- Focus on the materiality of the risk

- Identify the threats to the achievement of the business goals and objectives

Educational Objective 4

4-1. These are the organizational characteristics associated with a high level of risk assurance:

- The board of directors is certain that key risks that could affect the organization's successful attainment of goals and objectives have been properly identified, quantified, prioritized, and managed in an effective and cost-efficient manner.

- Managers have implemented a system of effective risk management controls; they also have an effective risk monitoring system in place and are using it.

- Risk reporting systems are providing information up the management chain to the board of directors, as well as down the management chain to the operating units.

- A culture of risk management prevails within the organization. Internally, employees recognize this culture; externally, customers, suppliers, lenders, and shareholders are aware of the organization's risk management culture as well.

4-2. These are examples of organizational sources of risk assurance:

- Policy and procedures documentation

- Normal business unit and department operating reports

- Internal audit reports of operations and processes, internal controls, and risk monitoring

- Risk management reports and documentation

4-3. These are examples of external sources of risk assurance:

- External audits

- Favorable press reports

- The willingness of lenders to supply funds at favorable rates

- Surveys of customers and suppliers

4-4. The purpose of the Control Risk Self-Assessment (CRSA) model is to evaluate the effectiveness of business processes.

4-5.   These are the benefits of risk assurance to internal and external stakeholders:

- The board of directors has greater confidence in management effectiveness.

- Employees have greater job security.

- Tensions are reduced within the organization.

- Customers and suppliers are more confident in the financial health and well-being of the organization.

- Lenders and equity shareholders have greater confidence in the organization.

- Insurance premiums and other hazard risk management costs are reduced.

- Regulatory authorities have greater trust in the organization.

4-6.   An internal audit can provide evidence that risk controls are in place and functioning as designed.

Educational Objective 5

5-1.   These are the key design features that risk management monitoring and reporting must incorporate:

- Risk reporting should direct to the appropriate people the information necessary to manage strategic, financial, and operational risks.

- Information reported from the lowest levels, whether quantitative or qualitative data, must be consolidated and integrated as it flows up to the board of directors.

- The information must be in an appropriate and easy-to-use format at every stage of reporting.

5-2.   Examples of reports generated by a risk monitoring and reporting system include risk response plans, financial reports, and incident reports.

5-3.   Effective risk reports should include objective measurements and subjective assessments and perspectives so that management's views and insights are clearly expressed. Reports should show trends, comparative performance measures, and compliance with standards. Both internal and external sources of information should be included in the reports.

5-4.   These are two kinds of choices to be aware of in managing the data reporting process:

- Integrated reporting versus silo reporting

- Quantitative data versus qualitative data

5-5.   These are features and concepts that some organizations find useful in a report format:

- Drill-down capability, which allows the user to view data at increasing levels of detail

- Current and updatable information, so that the user knows what is happening right now

- Room for analysis and commentary from the users at each level, so that additional information can be shared immediately

Exam Information

About Institutes Exams

Exam questions are based on the Educational Objectives stated in the course guide and textbook. The exam is designed to measure whether you have met those Educational Objectives. The exam does not necessarily test every Educational Objective. It tests over a balanced sample of Educational Objectives.

How to Prepare for Institutes Exams

What can you do to prepare for an Institutes exam? Students who pass Institutes exams do the following:

▶ Use the assigned study materials. Focus your study on the Educational Objectives presented at the beginning of each course guide assignment. Thoroughly read the textbook and any other assigned materials, and then complete the course guide exercises. Choose a study method that best suits your needs; for example, participate in a traditional class, online class, or informal study group; or study on your own. Use The Institutes' SMART Study Aids (if available) for practice and review. If this course has an associated SMART Online Practice Exams product, you will find an access code on the inside back cover of this course guide. This access code allows you to print a full practice exam and to take additional online practice exams that will simulate an actual credentialing exam.

▶ Become familiar with the types of test questions asked on the exam. The practice exam in this course guide or in the SMART Online Practice Exams product will help you understand the different types of questions you will encounter on the exam.

▶ Maximize your test-taking time. Successful students use the sample exam in the course guide or in the SMART Online Practice Exams product to practice pacing themselves. Learning how to manage your time during the exam ensures that you will complete all of the test questions in the time allotted.

Types of Exam Questions

The exam for this course consists of objective questions of several types.

The Correct-Answer Type

In this type of question, the question stem is followed by four responses, one of which is absolutely correct. Select the *correct* answer.

> Which one of the following persons evaluates requests for insurance to determine which applicants are accepted and which are rejected?
>
> a.   The premium auditor
>
> b.   The loss control representative
>
> c.   The underwriter
>
> d.   The risk manager

The Best-Answer Type

In this type of question, the question stem is followed by four responses, only one of which is best, given the statement made or facts provided in the stem. Select the *best* answer.

> Several people within an insurer might be involved in determining whether an applicant for insurance is accepted. Which one of the following positions is primarily responsible for determining whether an applicant for insurance is accepted?
>
> a.   The loss control representative
>
> b.   The customer service representative
>
> c.   The underwriter
>
> d.   The premium auditor

The Incomplete-Statement or Sentence-Completion Type

In this type of question, the last part of the question stem consists of a portion of a statement rather than a direct question. Select the phrase that *correctly* or *best* completes the sentence.

> Residual market plans designed for individuals who are unable to obtain insurance on their personal property in the voluntary market are called
>
> a. VIN plans.
>
> b. Self-insured retention plans.
>
> c. Premium discount plans.
>
> d. FAIR plans.

"All of the Above" Type

In this type of question, only one of the first three answers could be correct, or all three might be correct, in which case the best answer would be "All of the above." Read all the answers and select the *best* answer.

> When a large commercial insured's policy is up for renewal, who is likely to provide input to the renewal decision process?
>
> a. The underwriter
>
> b. The loss control representative
>
> c. The producer
>
> d. All of the above

"All of the following, EXCEPT:" Type

In this type of question, responses include three correct answers and one answer that is incorrect or is clearly the least correct. Select the *incorrect* or *least correct* answer.

> All of the following adjust insurance claims, EXCEPT:
>
> a. Insurer claim representatives
>
> b. Premium auditors
>
> c. Producers
>
> d. Independent adjusters